Oregon
Real Estate Pre-License
Brokerage

2nd Edition

Oregon Real Estate Pre-license Brokerage

Executive Editor: Sara Glassmeyer

Project Manager: Arlin Kauffman,
LEAP Publishing Services

Developmental Editor: Molly Armstrong-Paschal

Art and Cover Composition: Chris Dailey

Cover Image: ProSchools

For product information and technology assistance, contact us at
OnCourse Learning and Sales Support, 1-855-733-7239.
For permission to use material from this text or product.

Library of Congress Control Number: 2015951042

ISBN-10: 1629801380
ISBN-13: 978-1-62980-138-4

OnCourse Learning
3100 Cumberland Blvd, Suite 1450
Atlanta, GA 30339
USA

Visit us at **www.oncoursepublishing.com**

Printed in the United States of America
2 3 4 5 6 7 20 19 18 17 16

Oregon Advertising and Other Office Activities

Overview

This lesson focuses on how to develop marketing and advertising strategies. Public relations and advertising methods and principal broker supervision of advertising are discussed. Discussion of property development, counseling and consulting, and competitive market analyses concludes the lesson.

Objectives

Upon completion of this lesson, the student should be able to:

1. Describe and compare two marketing strategies for promoting company services.
2. Identify the elements and describe the benefits of developing a comprehensive public relations campaign.
3. Explain the principal broker's role in supervision of advertising by licensees.
4. Describe the functions of principal brokers acting as property developers.
5. Explain the purpose of real estate counseling and consulting activities.
6. Describe state license requirements for appraisal activity.
7. Describe restrictions on real estate licensees providing CMAs and letter opinions.

Marketing Basics

A real estate brokerage generally needs a multipronged marketing effort in the form of:

- public relations campaigns to make the public aware of the various different services the firm offers and to distinguish the firm from the competition.
- name recognition to draw clients and licensees to contact the brokerage for their services.
- advertising of the individual properties of its clients and different categories of properties for sale or lease, while adding to the public's image of the firm with complementary promotional materials.

----- MARKETING BASICS -----

Market Research

To adequately market its services, a brokerage will determine the needs of its market through market research. This can be done by contracting with a marketing firm, if the firm does not have a staff member who is expert at conducting such research. Once the initial research has been done, the principal broker or a selected employee or manager can keep it up to date.

Based on the research, the principal broker will develop methods to fill those needs, and then advertise and promote the company's services and the clients' products to the targeted market groups with a marketing plan that will help conserve funds in the advertising budget.

Target Markets

In marketing, the principal broker needs to focus on what are called the **4 P's of Marketing**:

1. Product
2. Price
3. Place
4. Promotion

The principal broker's **products** are the services he offers to clients and customers. Real estate advertising will stress the fact that the principal broker's agents are knowledgeable professionals able to assist in:

- finding the right property at the right price.
- marketing property to effect a speedy sale and closing at the right price.
- navigating through the steps required in a real estate transaction, saving the client from hassles and costly mistakes.

Price is the fee for the service provided that will produce the profit margin needed to stay in business. A principal broker must pay attention to competition, so that he does not price himself out of the market, while being cautious of not violating anti-trust laws.

Place refers to his place in the market. A principal broker needs to determine what segments of the market he will seek and the logistics involved in handling transactions for those segments. For instance, he would want to be close enough to support services, such as a title company, as well as to the real property he expects to handle.

Promotion involves ensuring that promotional efforts are adequate to communicate the principal broker's products and his clients' products to potential consumers.

Mass Marketing

Mass marketing is marketing to a large number of persons without having any knowledge of whether they have any interest in or need for the principal broker's

 services, such as mailing postcards to every household in a certain area. If done improperly to obtain business in the immediate future, this will waste a lot of money.

However, local real estate companies will support children's sports teams, parades, local fairs, and many other activities to generate name recognition, and national firms spend large amounts of money on "image" ads in order to keep the corporate name and logo in front of the public. The company **logo** is a symbol used with the company name to help the public quickly identify the company and project an image for a company. Successful examples are the Rock of Gibraltar used by Prudential to project its reliability and strength, and the swoosh used by Nike to project speed.

Segment Marketing

A more efficient use of the advertising budget may be **segment marketing**. With this strategy, the principal broker divides his chosen market into homogeneous groups, chooses which market segment he wishes to target, and spends a significant amount of his advertising dollar on capturing the segments he has chosen. This allows him to focus his marketing efforts on those who are most likely to use the firm's services. His segment may be:

- geographical, focusing on attracting clients based on the area's climate, geographic features (mountains, rivers, ocean, etc.), or infrastructure.
- demographic, focusing on certain age groups (first-time homebuyers, senior housing, etc.) or income groups.
- psychographic, focusing on particular attitudes and lifestyles.
- behavioral, relating to the different property types found in the area, the sensitivity to changing prices, and loyalty towards a professional used in the past (working with past clients).

Niche Marketing

Within the various marketing segments, a brokerage can seek to serve a **niche market**, such as the senior market. Such a principal broker would not only find appropriate housing for retirees, but also assist in the entire process of downsizing from the large family home to more manageable accommodations. This is a niche crying out for expert real estate help.

Another niche market is that of newly formed families with young children, who are currently renting. Agents may be able to offer forums to explain how they can afford to buy a home.

If the firm is the only brokerage within miles, the principal broker would be at an advantage if his market of choice is that specific area, unless the area had few sales or sales mostly by word of mouth.

Other potentially profitable niches might be:
- people moving into a retirement area.
- people looking to purchase a vacation home.
- fee for service.
- buyer brokerage.
- identifying property for national franchises to locate new retail outlets.

Agents' Skills

Agents within a firm may have widely diverse experiences and education, giving them access to different groups of individuals in different segments of the population. A good managing broker will be able to recognize the strengths and weaknesses of his agents. The managing broker should make every effort to guide an agent toward concentrating his marketing efforts on the niche that best matches his abilities and interests.

----- COMPETITION -----

A principal broker can equal or exceed the competition, even if his firm is new by:
- paying attention to industry trends.
- making use of different methods of market penetration.
- first noticing changes in the demographics in his market area (upper-end buyers attracted by new industry; tourism creating a new rental market; retirees creating a demand for new senior-living units).
- finding holes in the market that the competition has ignored or overlooked (perhaps the geographic area just beyond where a competitor stops his marketing efforts).

- finding the right package of services to offer (in a small town he may be expected to sell all types of real estate; in a large metropolitan area he may be expected to offer property management services to clients who purchase investment properties; in a particular area, he may be expected to advertise all listings every week in the local newspaper).

One major goal of a principal broker is to increase his market share. Assume there are three residential real estate brokerages (Brokers A, B, and C) in town. Last year 1,000 properties changed hands. Each brokerage handled 250 transactions (25% market share), and 250 were For Sale by Owner (FSBO). Market share can be increased by:
- maintaining sales volume when the overall market is depressed. This will not increase profits, but it may place the company in a very favorable position when the market recovers.
- increasing sales volume. If Broker A can increase its volume by 10%, to 275 transactions, it would have a market share 27.5%. To increase market share, Broker A will analyze the strengths and weaknesses of the competition and the FSBO market and then go after the potential client base of one or both of the other brokers, or he could promote his services to potential FSBOs.

Although they compete, residential brokerages also cooperate. To succeed in the business, a principal broker must be able to work with competitors and get them to work with him. To do this, he must offer them a fair share of his listing commission and not antagonize them.

Cooperating brokers can be offered a flat amount or a percentage of the sales price. This amount cannot be set by the MLS or any other group of brokers. It is set by each  individual company, based on what it feels is necessary to attract competitors to try to sell the company's listings. If most brokers in the area offer 3% of the sales price to the selling broker, the listing broker may find it difficult to satisfy his clients' needs by offering only 2.5%. Therefore, although no brokers agreed that they would pay each other 3%, most would offer around that percentage and would not be in violation of anti-trust laws.

Cooperation includes using the services a multiple listing service can offer, such as:
- sending e-mail to other agents directly from the multiple listing service's website.
- doing prospecting and reverse-prospecting, by inputting the needs of buyers and sellers into the MLS system.
- e-mailing property descriptions to clients and customers directly from the MLS.

A listing agent must take responsibility for entering information into the MLS database accurately and in a way that gets a favorable response from other agents, so they are more likely to promote and sell his listed property. He should stress to the sellers that the property needs to be uncluttered, neat, and clean, so that pictures in the MLS will show the property to its best advantage and showings have a greater likelihood of success. He should try to hold an open house for fellow real estate licensees as soon as possible after the listing is signed, when their curiosity is at its height. These open houses are as good an opportunity for networking as for showing the property that is listed.

One of the worst missteps a principal broker can make is to allow members of his firm to make remarks, justified or not, that belittle their competitors. The principal broker must be particularly watchful when an agent who has worked for the competition joins the firm. Because competitors will often become cooperators, there should never be any disparagement of them. Selling agents who are pleasant and professional in their dealings, will find their clients will be well served, because the listing agent will work harder to see that the transaction runs smoothly. Selling agents who have come to dislike the listing agent for remarks he may have made may decide not to show his listings.

----- PUBLIC RELATIONS -----

What It Is

Public relations refers to any word or action of the firm or its people that affects the firm's relationship with those who may influence its profitability and reputation.

The primary objectives of public relations are to:
- project a desired image.
- create a favorable public opinion and goodwill towards the firm, its associates and its method of operation.

A successful public relations program will involve making sure that every action of a representative of the firm and every word in print concerning the firm reflects the company's philosophy and matches the company's image to its marketing plan. This is extremely important because, once the public perceives the firm in a negative light, it is very difficult and very expensive to try to change that perception. This will adversely impact the firm's ability to recruit agents, attract buyers, and entice sellers to list.

In deciding on the type of public relations campaign to pursue, development of the company's image is of primary importance. The manager would first determine the image that is to be projected so he can design a campaign to foster that image. Applying the mission statement and the data derived from studying the customer and client base of the firm, the manager may decide to emphasize its expertise or its quality of service.

An existing real estate firm may want to project the image of being solid and having been in the community for a long time. A company that has been acquired and is "under new management" may need a facelift, centering its campaign on the firm's new web capabilities, allowing its agents to keep clients informed of every step of the home-buying or selling process. Throughout the campaign, care must be taken to reinforce the positive characteristics that made the company attractive to take over in the first place.

A manager may want to emphasize particular aspects that have become part of the firm's image over the years, such as the reliability, integrity, specialty niche, or a small-town caring attitude of the agents. For instance:

- "Our agents have a combined expertise of 200 years serving the valley."
- "We have helped over 1,000 people achieve their dream."
- "500 satisfied clients couldn't be wrong."
- "Our buyer representatives are here to serve only you."
- "No one knows the neighborhood better than us."

How to Do It

A principal broker can become known through his involvement in community affairs and concern for local problems by:

- becoming a cultural leader by sponsoring or participating in cultural events.
- running for political office.
- sponsoring sports teams or recreational groups.
- getting involved in service clubs in the community or having a staff member represent the firm in each major civic or service organization.
- providing refreshments, equipment, or staff support for local benefit programs.

A principal broker can generate goodwill among his service suppliers in order to get enhanced service from them by:

- showing recognition of their service.
- occasionally attending their group functions.
- taking them to lunch.
- learning how he can perform his functions in a way that makes their job easier.

A principal broker can also use the media to spread the word about his firm.

- He can use newspapers, magazines and the Internet to:
  o advertise his properties and his services.
  o generate publicity (information about the firm or its associates to attract public notice) by publicizing his involvement in community affairs, the hiring of new associates, or awards given to the firm or its associates, or by providing a publisher with news releases relating activities of importance to the readership.
  o show his expertise through feature articles, for instance, about the current real estate market or about what to look for in new construction or how to prepare a home for showing.
- He might use television to:
  o show homes he has listed for sale.
  o participate in discussions of real estate matters with which he has expert knowledge.

- He might participate in or host a radio real estate talk show.
- He might hand out or mail flyers or other printed material directly to prospects or to an entire area, promoting the company's services, reprinting news releases or feature articles, promoting listed properties, or providing information about the real estate market.
- He might give talks to community organizations and service clubs on topics in which he has expert knowledge.
- He might have an occasional open house for suppliers, clients and cooperators, to show appreciation for their business and/or service to the firm.

What to Expect

Public relations campaigns will not produce instantaneous results. They may generate some contacts, but these may not result in increased business for months. However, the marketing manager should attempt to evaluate the results of any public relations program against the firm's stated objectives.

----- PROMOTION AND ADVERTISING -----

Direct efforts to make people contact the company for its services would constitute advertising and promotion.

Promotion

A number of name recognition and marketing techniques have proven successful.

A blitz ad campaign is helpful in initial publicity and advertising for a new office or for turning around an existing, low-producing office, whether a franchise or an independent brokerage. This involves placing ads in a multitude of publications and media, repeating  the same general message in each ad in order to achieve name recognition and word-of-mouth promotion. The message may be to publicize the experience of the sales force, create a positive image in the minds of the public, and bring the office to the attention of potential cooperating firms.

Location, or strategic placement, of the firm's ads in magazines may be important. The order of preferential position, reflected by the cost of an ad in each location, is front cover, back cover, inside front cover and inside back cover. However, it would be advisable to inquire of customers and clients where they heard the principal broker's name and why they contacted the firm. Often it is referrals from prior clients or the location of the office that made the difference, and the extra money spent for the premium location of the firm's advertising may be misspent.

A number of companies have added words such as "exclusively" or "only" on For Sale signs to promote their name recognition. While this may confuse some buyers into believing they must use that firm to buy the listed house, it is not considered unethical or illegal (since the principal broker does have an exclusive agency or exclusive right-to-sell listing), and may be effective.

For companies and licensees who work solely or primarily on a referral basis, marketing is designed to effectively farm their referral base, so it will not dry up and so the competition will be not able to step in and take their clients and customers.

Licensees who develop a niche to practice as buyer representatives exclusively, and never as listing agents or as dual or disclosed limited agents, will have their marketing designed to point out the advantages of this practice.

Advertising

All advertising should adhere to the basic advertising formula: **AIDA**.

Advertising Basics – AIDA	
A	Attention
I	Interest
D	Desire
A	Action

An ad should attract **attention**. Something about the ad should stand out so the viewer will take time to read it. Things that can make an ad stand out include:
- an illustration.
- blank space.
- a bold border.
- unusual fonts.
- a headline. In the classified section, this is what readers most often use to screen ads they will read. It should focus attention on the feature of the property or terms of sale that will most appeal to a potential buyer.

The ad should point out features to arouse the reader's interest, generally in order of their appeal. If there is enough space, it should contain descriptive adjectives and persuasive words to appeal to the reader's emotions.

It should create a desire on the part of the reader to want to see the property and incite the reader to take action quickly. The best ads are those that will elicit a phone call, e-mail, Internet query, or appearance at an open house.

Many principal brokers feel it is important to advertise properties every week in the real estate section of the newspaper, just to keep the firm's name in front of the public. Others also advertise listed properties in one or more real estate magazines. Still others, generally the large franchise companies, distribute their own magazines throughout the community. What is important for principal brokers to remember, though, is that consistent use of a theme or an image or logo that keeps the company in the public's memory is often more important than the frequency of ads.

In order to advertise the name and image of the brokerage, firms use an amazing number of venues. These include the following:
- Cable or local television and radio ads promoting properties or broker services
- Billboards
- Promotional gifts with the company name, phone number, and logo
- Handouts
- Repeated mailings to new or repeat customers (These can be newsletters, recipes, brochures, maps, or such novelties as stamps, flower seeds, candy corn, or other little reminders sent every six weeks or so to core clients, or those they want to be core.)
- Yellow page ads
- Newspaper classified and display ads
- Business cards, stationery, For Sale signs, brochures, and flyers with the company logo
- Internet

For Sale Signs
One of the most effective forms of advertising is the For Sale sign.
- It communicates to the world that the property is for sale.
- It may arouse interest in those who have not been actively looking for a house. It allows neighbors, who probably like the neighborhood, to spread the word about the listing.
- It may prompt a neighbor to list with that firm or licensee.
- It is silent, continuous, and recyclable.
- It keeps the principal broker's name in front of public.
- When the property is sold, the "Sold" sticker is evidence that the principal broker or licensee successfully completed his job (even if he did not directly make the sale).

For greatest effect, the signs should be clean and attractive. The licensee needs to assure signs are placed legally on the property with the owner's consent.

Internet Advertising

The Internet is a very attractive medium for obtaining clients and customers. Principal brokers may use web pages for marketing themselves and advertising their listings and the listings of other licensees. Some agents have one or more pages at their company's website. Others create their own website with their own domain name.

When designing a business web page, it is important to include pertinent and beneficial information to those who visit the site. A sample of a number of real estate agent websites would reveal that the most user-friendly sites provide:

- market facts.
- loan information.
- qualifying information.
- information about the agent and the company.
- other information to cause prospective homebuyers or sellers to want to periodically visit the site.

The Internet also enables agents to use e-mail in marketing their properties and services. Upon listing a property, the licensee can almost instantaneously e-mail a flyer and other information to other agents as well as to prospective buyers.

Newspaper Advertising

Classified advertising is a common form of real property advertising. The ads are in columnar form in a separate section of the newspaper. The principal broker can either place all listings in one long ad, which costs less because he only has to place his firm's name and phone number once, or place each property in its own section, with the firm's name showing in each ad.

Display advertising is placed in the feature section of a newspaper and most often includes one or more photographs. Frequently, this type of ad is used for expensive properties or to announce a new associate.

A principal broker who advertises many properties, and often, will be able to take advantage of discounts:

- Open rates, paid by advertisers who sporadically place advertisements, are the highest rates.
- Contract rates provide discounts for an agreement to place a certain number of lines of advertising.
- Space contracts base discounts on an agreement to buy a specific amount of space over a specified period of time.
- Time contracts provide a discount in return for an agreement to run a minimum number of ads over a specified period of time.

To Improve Effectiveness of Advertising

→ On the average, an ad needs to be viewed three times before a sale is made.

→ While frequency is important, the creativity and power of the ad itself are equally important.

→ Color in an ad makes a difference.

→ Location in the publication is important. The order of preferential position is front cover, back cover, inside front cover, and inside back cover.

→ The use of inserted flyers increases exposure.

→ Include the price; it is an automatic qualifier.

→ A picture is worth a thousand words.

→ A larger ad is better.

→ A second ad in the same publication increases readership by an average of 15%.

Policies, Supervision and Laws

----- ADVERTISING POLICIES AND SUPERVISION -----

If a principal broker can establish an effective advertising policy, he can minimize the expense of advertising listed property and aid associates in publishing more effective ads. Associates need to know the objectives for the firm's advertising, so they can understand when, why, and how much money the brokerage will spend on advertising. The advertising goal has to be clear: to get the targeted audience to make an appointment to see the property that was advertised or one with similar characteristics.

A reasonable advertising budget will pay for advertising the firm's listings as well as public relations and promotion of the firm. Even though many brokerage firms charge their agents for advertising listed properties, most firms will pay for at least one open house ad or an occasional advertising spread.

Quite often, escrow companies, title companies, and mortgage brokers and lenders are willing to advertise on the same page of a glossy real estate magazine as the brokerage.

This is particularly important when the principal broker is just beginning because the principal broker will be able to place ads each month for a reasonable amount of money, and those months when he has a great number of properties listed, he can purchase more pages.

The main consideration in determining how much to spend on advertising for a particular property should be the characteristics of the listing itself, including the asking price, the commission, and the number of similar properties listed by the firm. Ads that are not too specific can be directed at more than one type of buyer. When a limited number of ads will be placed in a publication, the principal broker will want to choose a variety of styles and price ranges, so a variety of prospective buyers will be enticed to call.

Once an ad has been approved, there should be a separate page in the ad book showing each ad for that day and an explanatory paragraph to help any agent on floor answer questions about the properties. It is also helpful to have a notation of competing properties. That way if there is a call on a listing that is not quite what the caller is looking for, the person taking the call can "convert" that caller into a buyer for another property.

The listing agent should record the dates of all ads and the places the ads appeared. It is important to:
- keep track of how many calls were elicited from each ad.
- notify the sellers of the results of the advertising campaign for their properties. This will:
  - show them the efforts put into selling their properties.
  - help the agent get an extension of the listing, if needed.
  - help show the seller the need to lower the listing price or offer better terms or conditions to buyers, if market conditions indicate such action is needed.

Whoever answers floor calls should complete a call log showing:
- the listing called on.
- where the caller learned about the listing.
- the name and phone number of the caller.

By reviewing the logs, the principal broker can analyze which ads are effective and which agents are able to turn a caller from a curious information seeker to an appointment.

Supervision

Anyone may prepare an ad, including an unlicensed personal assistant. A licensee may develop his own website or design his own business cards. In all cases, however, the principal broker is ultimately responsible for the advertising. While the principal broker may delegate direct supervisory authority over advertising originating in a branch office to the branch office manager, he remains responsible for all advertising done under his real estate license.

To comply with all requirements, the principal broker or the branch manager needs to establish and implement procedures for reviewing all advertising to ensure it:
- complies with the license law and other statutes. For instance, the ad must be in the principal broker's licensed name (i.e., the company name).
- is consistent with company policy. For instance, company policy may be to include amenities and price, but not financing terms.
- is addressed to the target market. For instance, an ad on a property in county A might not reach the desired audience if it is run in a local newspaper in county B.
- complies with the requirements of federal, state, and local fair housing laws by not implying a limitation to a protected class.
- does not include an offer to share commissions. For instance, an offer of services free of charge that would be tied to or contingent upon a service for which the licensee would be compensated would create an illegal sharing of commissions.

- does not misrepresent any material facts about the property, terms of sale offered, property values, or services provided by the firm. The principal broker may want to see documentation of facts about the property that are included in the ad; assure the price advertised is that agreed upon by the owner; and ensure the ad does not create a misleading impression, resulting in misrepresentation by omission.

The Internet poses a number of potential problems for a principal broker. It makes it easy for agents to develop their own personal web pages, allowing the public and other licensees to contact them without going through the principal broker. Yet the principal broker is responsible for reasonable supervision of the web pages and the Internet use of all of his licensees. If the principal broker does not adequately supervise the activities of the licensee who owns the website, he is in violation of the law.

To effectively handle this supervisory responsibility, the principal broker should:
- set an office policy on the use of personal web pages by associated licensees and the placement of listing information on the Internet.
- make reasonable efforts to review and approve all information that will be placed on any personal web page, make sure that information on the Internet does not become dated, and that errors in information are corrected in a timely manner.

----- OREGON ADVERTISING -----

The Oregon Administrative Rules (OAR 863-015-0125) regulate the advertising of licensees. Advertising is defined as "advertising activity conducted by mail, telephone, the Internet, the World Wide Web, email, electronic bulletin board or other similar electronic common carrier systems, business cards, signs, billboards, and telephonic greetings or answering machines. The list contained in the rule is not exclusive because "advertising" includes "all forms of representation, promotion and solicitation disseminated in any manner and by any means of communication for any purpose related to professional real estate activity." In short, if a licensee is making information about property, or even themselves and their company available to the public, to a member of the public, or even to other agents, they are advertising. According to Oregon courts, any statement by a licensee in any form is a violation of license law if the statement is "of such a character as reasonably to induce any person to act to his damage or injury."

According to the Administrative Rules, a licensee must meet the following criteria when advertising:
- When a licensee includes their name in advertising, they must use either their licensed name or a common derivative of their name such as "Bob" for Robert.
- The licensed name or registered business name of the principal broker must be prominently displayed, immediately noticeable and conspicuous in all advertising.
- With limited exceptions, a principal broker must review the advertising of associated brokers and property managers, and is responsible for all advertising approved by the principal broker that bears their name. A branch manager

principal broker may supervise advertising in the branch with written permission of the principal broker.

Advertising in electronic media or by electronic means must meet certain specific requirements:

- The first page (of a web page, for example) the licensed name of the principal broker or his registered business name. The page must also include a statement that the licensee is licensed in Oregon. It would be a good idea for licensee to put that statement in a signature in their outgoing e-mails.
- Sponsored links such as MLS advertising do not have to have this information, but when the consumer clicks on the link the webpage he is taken to must have it.

The rules also contain a provision that "no advertising may guarantee future profits."

The last provision deals with advertising using the term "team" or "group". It says that a team or group name cannot be deceptively similar to a trademarked name. At least one of the team must be licensed and that all licensed members of the team or group are associated with the same principal broker and they must use their licensed names. If unlicensed persons are named it must be noted that they are not licensed.

----- OTHER LAWS -----

Marketing and advertising may also entail telephone solicitations, or cold calling. A licensee can no longer just pick up a phone and call every person on a street or on a page in the phone book without risking serious legal repercussions. There are two laws of significance regarding telephone solicitations.

One is a law prohibiting the use of fax machines and automatic dialing and announcing devices (computer phone calls) to solicit business by phone. The statute does, however, allow the use of such machines in calling any party with whom the licensee has an existing business relationship.

The second law provides that consumers may list their names and phone numbers on a federal "no call" list. Telephone solicitors (a term which includes real estate agents) must avoid calling persons on that list unless they have established business relationships. However, calls can be made to persons on the "no call" list for up to 18 months after a business transaction has been completed with them (such as former clients) and for up to three months after they have made an inquiry (such as persons who called on ads). This exception terminates if they ask that they not be called any longer.

----- Truth in Advertising -----

Advertising laws are aimed at protecting consumers by requiring advertisers to be truthful, and substantiate all claims made. Failure to comply with advertising rules can result in lawsuits and civil penalties. The Federal Trade Commission (FTC) is the federal agency that enforces advertising. The FTC says that:

- Advertising must be truthful and non-deceptive.
- advertisers must be able to back up their claims.
- advertisements cannot be unfair.

There are prohibitions against bait and switch advertising such as knowingly keeping a sold listing on a website as actively on the market, so the licensee can receive calls and say to the prospect: "I am sorry that property is not available now, but I can show you a nearby property."

Calling what is really a three bedroom home with a den and no closet a "four bedroom" home, could be considered deceptive advertising.

Other Office Activities

Real estate brokers may engage in activities other than sales, such as construction and development, counseling and consulting, and provision of competitive market analyses. Principal brokers need to make sure that all activities are performed in compliance with the law and regulations, only by persons competent to perform them, and only under his supervision.

----- PROPERTY DEVELOPMENT -----

Property development involves constructing improvements on real estate, such as providing gas, water and sewage lines, digging, building structures, etc. The goal of a property developer is to supply the type and price range of real estate products that will meet and satisfy the demand in the marketplace.

A broker who is inexperienced in development and subdividing may gain experience and lessen his risks by:
- persuading the landowner to hire the broker as a subdivider on a managed plan.
- entering into a partnership with one partner putting up the capital and the land and the other the management and merchandising skill.
- entering into a joint venture with others, sharing the risks and expenses.
- acting as a wholesaler of lots to be developed by a developer or investment group.

Some developers will only engage in **subdividing** the land, converting raw land into finished lots by installing improvements on and off the site, and then selling the lots to builders to complete the development. On the other hand, developer-builders will plan and complete the entire subdivision through the sale of the last home in a subdivision.

A broker involved in subdividing needs to carefully analyze the market and confirm with the local planning agency the likelihood of final approval of a proposed project for its intended use before making a firm commitment to buy property for development or subdividing. His marketing and financing plan must take into account state and local government regulations based on the Subdivision and Series Partition Control Law, administered by the Real Estate Commissioner, and the Subdivision and Partition Law, administered by city or county officials.

Property Development Regulation

A builder or subdivider who is a broker is regulated by the Real Estate Agency in the purchase and sale of his properties. If he has more than a 5% interest in the company owning the property and participates in the negotiations for the sale of the property, or if he owns the property in his own name, he must:

- disclose in writing, in the sale agreement, that he is licensed and representing himself as the seller in the transaction.
- place earnest money in a trust account or escrow.
- supervise the sales activity of any licensees working for him.
- maintain records for at least six years.

A broker associated with a principal broker must disclose his license status and have the transaction supervised by his principal broker as if it were a transaction conducted for a client.

----- COUNSELING AND CONSULTING -----

One of the niches in the real estate profession is real estate counseling. While a person does not need a real estate broker or principal broker license to advise, counsel, consult, or analyze in connection with permissible land use alternatives, environmental impact, building and use permit procedures, he does need the license to advise, counsel, consult, or analyze in connection with the acquisition or sale of real estate by an entity whose purpose is investment in real estate.

Counseling involves advising and guiding clients to help them make informed real estate decisions, rather than assisting them in any negotiations in a transaction. The function of the counselor is to help the client determine his goals, gather facts, analyze the data, recommend a course of action based on the client's goals, and then help the client carry out the course of action he has chosen.

A licensee must be capable of interpreting the financial statements of his potential clients so he may price property properly and judge the financial ability of a potential client to make a transaction. He must also be capable of applying the concept of the **time value of money**. This concept is that a dollar today is worth more than a dollar in the future. How much more is a matter for analysis. Knowledge of present value techniques is needed to value specific aspects of a transaction and to advise clients of the scenarios that best fit their needs.

A counselor must be capable of performing a real estate market analysis. This is a study of factors which contribute to the demand for and supply of a particular type of property. It allows the analyst to match demand with supply and helps him determine the highest and best use for a site and the price at which it should sell.

When advising investors on potential development sites, counselors must be aware of government factors and research zoning, building codes, availability of utilities, and ecological impacts. If a property is not zoned to allow the intended use, it will have to be rezoned. Counselors must also consider building codes. When an architect designs a project, he must adhere to local, state, and national building guidelines.

Commercial transactions can involve a large number of lease provisions that need to be understood by a counselor. Just as the commercial transaction is negotiable, the lease provisions are negotiable. Knowledge of the ramifications of lease provisions is required. An example would be the definition of space. The definition of space may influence how much rent a lessee will pay. Rent is usually charged on a square-foot basis. When the space rented is quoted as usable space, typically inside-wall to inside-wall, there is less square area charged for rent than there would be if the rent were charged based on rentable space. Space quoted as rentable space would include utility rooms, common area lobbies, hallways, and restrooms and is, therefore, larger. As such, usable space would have a higher cost per square foot than rentable space.

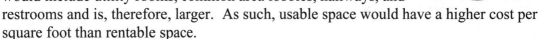

Counseling and Consulting Regulation

There are a number of regulations that apply to counseling and consulting by licensees.

When promoting one's services as a counselor or a consultant, the licensee must be sure his materials are truthful and not deceptive or misleading. This includes not using any words that state or imply that he is qualified or has a level of expertise other than that which he actually has. In other words, if he has no extensive experience to serve as the basis of his advice, he may have a difficult time justifying his claim that he is a consultant. Another concern is that the licensee acting as a counselor does not overextend his authorization and engage in unlicensed appraisal activity or offer legal or accounting advice which he is unqualified to give.

Furthermore, a principal broker must directly supervise all licensees associated with the brokerage in the fulfillment of their duties and obligations to their respective clients, under a written company policy. Therefore, if the licensees are to offer fee-for-service or consulting services, this activity should be authorized and controlled by the terms of the company policy manual or independent contractor agreement. The principal broker must also review, initial and date any document of agreement with a client within seven banking days after it has been accepted to ensure the licensee is capable of performing the tasks set forth in the agreement.

One of the services offered residential buyers and sellers by fee-for-service agents is a competitive market analysis (CMA). While agents who provide full service generally do not charge for a CMA, those who charge a fee rather than a commission will charge for a CMA either separately or as part of a package of services. There are a number of laws and rules with which the agent must comply in performing this activity.

A broker can provide competitive market analyses and letter opinions in the normal course of his business where he is giving an opinion, whether or not for a fee, either:

- in pursuit of a listing.
- to assist a potential purchaser in formulating an offer.
- to provide a broker's price opinion.

The license law defines a **competitive market analysis** as a method or process used in pursuing a listing agreement or in formulating an offer to acquire real estate in a transaction for the sale, lease, lease-option, or exchange of real estate. A competitive market analysis may:

- be expressed as an opinion of the value of the real estate in a contemplated transaction.
- include an analysis of market conditions, public records, past transactions and current listings of real estate.

A real estate licensee can provide a lending collateral analysis or default collateral analysis only if:

- the analysis is used only for the internal purposes of a financial institution; and
- in the case of a lending collateral analysis, the loan transaction at issue is less than $250,000.

As with all other professional real estate activities, CMAs and letter opinions, when provided by a broker, are under the control and supervision of the principal broker, and any fee charged for the letter opinion, competitive market analysis, or taxpayer representation must be paid through the principal broker.

Brain Teaser

Reinforce your understanding of the material by correctly completing the following sentences:

1. The company _____ is a symbol used with the company name to help the public quickly identify the company and project an image for a company.

2. _____ _____ refers to any word or action of the firm or its people that affects the firm's relationship with those who may influence its profitability and reputation.

3. All advertising should adhere to the basic advertising formula – _____.

4. Calls can be made to persons on the "no call" list for up to _____ months after a business transaction has been completed with them and for up to _____ months after they have made an inquiry.

5. A _____ _____ analysis is a method or process used in pursuing a listing agreement or in formulating an offer to acquire real estate in a transaction for the sale, lease, lease-option, or exchange of real estate.

Brain Teaser Answers

1. The company **logo** is a symbol used with the company name to help the public quickly identify the company and project an image for a company.

2. **Public relations** refers to any word or action of the firm or its people that affects the firm's relationship with those who may influence its profitability and reputation.

3. All advertising should adhere to the basic advertising formula – **AIDA**.

4. Calls can be made to persons on the "no call" list for up to **18** months after a business transaction has been completed with them and for up to **three** months after they have made an inquiry.

5. A **competitive market** analysis is a method or process used in pursuing a listing agreement or in formulating an offer to acquire real estate in a transaction for the sale, lease, lease-option, or exchange of real estate

Review – Oregon Advertising and Other Office Activities

This lesson focuses on advertising strategies, principal broker supervision of advertising, property development, counseling and consulting, and competitive market analyses.

Marketing

A real estate brokerage generally needs a marketing effort in the form of public relations campaigns, name recognition to draw clients and licensees, and advertising of individual properties.

In marketing, the broker needs to focus on the 4 P's of Marketing: product, price, place and promotion. The broker's products are the services he offers to clients and customers. Price is the fee for the service provided that will produce the profit margin needed to stay in business. Place refers to his place in the market. Promotion involves ensuring that promotional efforts are adequate to communicate the broker's products and his clients' products to potential consumers.

Mass marketing is marketing to a large number of persons without having any knowledge of whether they have any interest in or need for the broker's services, such as mailing postcards to every household in a certain area. The company logo is a symbol used with the company name to help the public quickly identify the company and project an image for a company.

Segment marketing allows the broker to focus his marketing efforts on those who are most likely to use the firm's services.

Public Relations

Public relations refers to any word or action of the firm or its people that affects the firm's relationship with those who may influence its profitability and reputation. The primary objectives of public relations are to project a desired image and create a favorable public opinion and goodwill towards the firm, its associates and its method of operation.

Advertising

A blitz ad campaign is helpful in initial publicity and advertising for a new office or for turning around an existing, low-producing office, whether a franchise or an independent brokerage.

Location, or strategic placement, of the firm's ads in magazines may be important. The order of preferential position, reflected by the cost of an ad in each location, is front cover, back cover, inside front cover and inside back cover.

All advertising should adhere to the basic advertising formula: AIDA. An ad should attract attention. The ad should point out features to arouse the reader's interest, generally in order of their appeal. The ad should create a desire on the part of the reader to want to see the property and incite the reader to take action quickly. The best ads are those that will elicit a phone call, e-mail, Internet query, or appearance at an open house.

Policy and Supervision

The principal broker should set an office policy on the use of personal web pages by associated licensees and the placement of listing information on the Internet, make reasonable efforts to review and approve all information that will be placed on any personal web page, make sure that information on the Internet does not become dated, that errors in information are corrected in a timely manner, and ensure that any licensee providing virtual tours featuring the inside of homes has the express written permission of the owner to do so.

"No Call" Restrictions

Telephone solicitors must avoid calling persons on the "no call" list unless they have established business relationships. Calls can be made to persons on the list for up to 18 months after a business transaction has been completed with them and for up to three months after they have made an inquiry.

Other Office Activities

The brokers may engage in activities other than sales, such as construction and development, counseling and consulting, and the provision of competitive market analyses. Principal brokers need to ensure that all activities are performed in compliance with the law and regulations, only by persons competent to perform them, and only under his supervision.

A broker involved in subdividing needs a marketing and financing plan that takes into account state and local government regulations. He is also regulated by the Real Estate Agency in the purchase and sale of his properties, if he has more than a 5% interest in the company owning the property and participates in the negotiations for the sale of the property or if he owns the property in his own name.

The function of a real estate counselor is to help the client determine his goals, gather facts, analyze the data, recommend a course of action based on the client's goals, and then help the client carry out the course of action he has chosen. When promoting one's services as a counselor or a consultant, the licensee must not use any words that state or imply that he is qualified or has a level of expertise, other than that he actually has, and must not overextend his authorization and engage in unlicensed appraisal activity or offer legal or accounting advice which he is unqualified to give.

A broker can provide competitive market analyses and letter opinions in the normal course of his business, where he is giving an opinion, whether or not for a fee, either in pursuit of a listing, to assist a potential purchaser in formulating an offer, or to provide a broker's price opinion. CMAs and letter opinions by a broker are under the control and supervision of the principal broker, and any fee charged for the letter opinion, competitive market analysis, or taxpayer representation must be paid through the principal broker.

Oregon Closings and Records

Overview

This lesson starts with an explanation of the calculations involved in preparing a closing statement. It concludes with a discussion of a broker's recordkeeping requirements.

Objectives

Upon completion of this lesson, the student should be able to:

1. Identify and describe the significant elements of a settlement statement including purchase price and earnest money deposit, financing, loan payoffs, closing costs, prorations, sales commissions, buyer's cash requirements and seller's proceeds.
2. Identify a buyer's and a seller's credits and debits in closing.
3. Explain how closing dates and different financing methods affect closing costs.
4. Demonstrate how taxes and insurance are handled at closing, including proration, prepayment and reserve accounts.
5. Perform tax and interest prorates.
6. List the types of records brokers must maintain.
7. Explain the requirements for principal broker retention of records.

Closer Responsibilities

----- CLOSER'S RESPONSIBILITY -----

The transfer of money from the buyer to the seller and of title from the seller to the buyer is accomplished through a process called **closing**. A principal broker has certain obligations to fulfill with regard to closings of real estate transactions.

A listing agreement does not obligate the listing principal broker to close a real estate transaction. According to the terms of the listing agreement, the principal broker has earned his commission when he has produced a buyer whose offer meets the price and terms of the listing, or whose offer is accepted by the seller, not when he closes the paperwork for the transaction.

However, to protect the seller, the administrative rules require that the principal broker who is the listing broker in a transaction promptly close the transaction, unless all parties to the transaction agree in writing to delegate the closing function to someone else, such as an escrow agent, an attorney, or another broker engaged in the transaction. This rule does not require or even recommend that the principal broker close the transaction. Its purpose is only to make sure that, if the parties cannot agree to have someone else handle that function, he must do so, and promptly. If the principal broker does close the transaction, in effect he is performing escrow services.

Normally a person performing escrow services is required to be licensed as an escrow agent. However, a principal broker may act as an escrow agent without obtaining an escrow agent license when he performs the closing for the principals in a transaction in which he participated as a broker and the principals are not charged a separate fee for the escrow services. If a principal broker does close the transaction, he cannot collect or charge a fee for the closing service unless he has an escrow agent license. Therefore, if a principal broker were to close a transaction, he must do so for no compensation or first obtain an escrow agent's license.

In Oregon, very few transactions are closed by brokers. Most are closed by licensed escrow agents who have the time and expertise to properly handle this function and who relieve the principal broker of the liability for the closing. In Oregon, an escrow agent may accept funds into escrow only with dated written instructions or a dated written agreement between the parties, with or without the services of a real estate licensee. Escrow may then review legal documents for accuracy and typographical errors and may disburse funds as authorized by both principals. They however, cannot draft legal documents or perform a legal review of them.

If a principal broker conducts a closing, he must ensure that the buyer and the seller each receive a complete detailed closing statement showing the amount and purpose of all receipts, adjustments and disbursements. He must also retain a copy of the closing statement, showing all receipts, disbursements and adjustments, and signed by the seller or sellers and buyer or buyers, for six years. He will be held personally liable for any errors in computations or any negligence in failing to determine the true facts in every element affecting the transaction.

A principal broker who accepts the closing responsibility can delegate the function to a broker associated with him. To do so, he must:

- provide to that associated broker written authorization to handle the closing function.
- file a copy of the authorization bearing his signature with the Real Estate Commissioner.
- directly supervise the associated broker's handling of the closing function.

Without this written authorization and the principal broker's direct supervision, the licensee cannot handle the closing function. The licensee does not need authorization from either the buyer or the seller in the transaction, nor does he need approval of the authorization by the Real Estate Agency (the Agency). Since the buyer and seller and the Agency do not know his capability to close a transaction, they are not required to give authorization or approval. If he handles the function poorly, he and the principal broker will be responsible for any incompetence or negligence.

----- CLOSING STATEMENT -----

A **closing statement** is the written evidence of the monetary history of a real estate transaction. A **buyer's closing statement** presents the buyer's closing costs and credits in detail so that he will know what is expected of him at closing. The **seller's closing statement** provides the seller with a complete accounting of his own closing costs and credits and the amount of money he will receive from the proceeds of the sale.

In any real estate transaction, there are **closing** (or **settlement**) **costs**. These are moneys that the buyer and seller pay to close the transaction. What is included, the amount, and who pays depends on the transaction and its terms, the existence of any liens against the parties or the real estate, and the type of financing to be used in the sale. In a transaction with conventional financing, the party responsible for payment of various closing costs is determined by agreement of the parties.

In the accounting performed on a closing statement, the buyer and seller each have a series of debits (charges) and credits.

The Buyer

The **buyer's debits** (charges) are all amounts due and payable at the time of closing, to the seller and others. They are amounts the buyer owes the seller and amounts to pay closing and loan costs (but not the loan itself) on the day of closing. Every check written by the closing agent (such as to pay closing costs) to be paid out of the buyer's closing account is a debit.

Amounts owed the seller include:
- the purchase price.
- a pro rata share of rents due but not collected, if the property is rental property.
- a pro rata share of items prepaid by the seller, such as prepaid property taxes.

In the case of unpaid rent, the buyer would owe the seller for the time from the last rent payment to closing. In the case of prepaid taxes, the buyer would owe the seller for the period from the day of closing through June 30, the end of the tax year.

Closing costs may include:
- the premium for a new property insurance policy.
- fees for recording the deed and the trust deed for a new loan.
- payment of any outstanding judgments against the buyer.
- in most cases, half of the escrow fee.

Loan costs include:
- the amount needed to fund a tax and insurance reserve account.
- the cost of a lender's title policy.
- a tax registration fee.
- the initial mortgage insurance premium charge.
- an assumption fee, if he is assuming the seller's existing loan.
- a loan origination fee.
- any fees for a survey, appraisal, or credit report, not paid outside of closing.
- interest on a new loan to the end of the month of closing.

The **buyer's credits** are what he uses to pay his debits. They include:
- any checks or cash deposited before or at closing.
- any financing used to pay the purchase price.
- amounts owed him by the seller.

Therefore, the buyer's credits include his earnest money deposit and the check or cash he needs to close. The amount he pays to close is determined by subtracting all other credits from the total of his debits.

> **For Example**
>
> If the buyer is to pay $350,000 cash for a property and had already paid $13,000 as earnest money, his check would be $337,000 at closing. The price would be a debit, and the earnest money and check to close would be credits.

Another credit to the buyer is the amount of financing, whether it is the current balance of a loan being assumed, a new loan from a third-party lender, or the amount of a land sales contract from, or purchase money mortgage (or trust deed) given to, the seller.

The buyer also is credited (and the seller is debited) for any amounts the seller owes him. This includes interest on an outstanding loan being assumed from the date of the last payment to the date of closing, as well as a prorated share of unpaid property taxes from July 1 to the date of closing.

It also includes all security deposits and fees received from current tenants; and a prorated share of rents received by the seller prior to the closing, which covers a period after closing.

> **For Example**
>
> If rent were collected on May 1 for the month of May, and the closing was held on May 15, the buyer is entitled to half the rent (that portion which covers the period from May 15 to June 1). Also, if rent for the final month of the lease had been collected, the buyer is entitled to that. If the seller had obtained a security deposit or cleaning fee, he must turn these over to the buyer, since it is the buyer who must refund this money to the tenants or use the money for its intended purpose at the conclusion of the lease.

The Seller

The **seller's credits** are amounts the buyer owes him on the day of closing. This is typically just the sales price and reimbursement of prepaid taxes. For the seller, any item that is paid into his closing account is a credit.

His debits reflect how his credits are disbursed on the day of closing. The debits reflect how the funds owed him are to be disbursed. Any item that is paid out of his account, even if paid to him, at closing, is a charge or debit.

Debits include the amount of any financing with which he is involved, closing costs, amounts he owes the buyer, and the check for the sales proceeds.

The financing debits include the balance of an existing loan being paid off or assumed by the buyer at closing, as well as the interest accrued on that loan since the last mortgage payment; or the amount of any land sales contract or purchase money mortgage used to help the buyer finance the purchase.

Typical seller closing costs are:
- the cost of the owner's title policy warranting title for the buyer.
- the broker's commission to the broker.
- the cost of recording documents to satisfy liens or otherwise clear title.
- half the escrow fee.

The seller also is debited (and the buyer is credited) for any amounts he owes the buyer. These include:

- interest on an outstanding loan being assumed from the date of the last payment to the date of closing.
- a prorated share of unpaid property taxes from July 1 to the date of closing.
- all security deposits and fees received from current tenants.
- a prorated share of rents received prior to the closing, which covers a period after closing.

The final debit for the seller is the amount he will actually receive from the closing. This is determined by subtracting all other charges from his credits.

----- SETTLEMENT ITEMS -----

The selling price is the price agreed to in the sales contract between the buyer and the seller. This is both a charge (debit) to the buyer and a credit to the seller.

If the buyer and seller agree that the buyer will purchase some items of personal property such as drapes, refrigerator, etc., for a price which is not included in the sales price, the price for the personal property increases the amount due from the buyer and the amount to be paid the seller. Therefore, it is a debit to the buyer and a credit to the seller.

Anything the buyer uses to pay off the sales price is a credit to the buyer, including:

- earnest money.
- new loan obtained from a lender.
- purchase money mortgage given to the seller.
- contract for deed (real estate contract) taken from the seller.
- loan assumed by the buyer.
- check from the buyer.

Some of these items are also debits to the seller, while some do not even appear on the seller's closing statement.

For Example

Earnest money paid by the buyer, whether cash or other property, is a credit to the buyer. If the earnest money is cash, it would not appear on the seller's statement, as it neither increases nor decreases the amount of cash the seller receives at closing. If, however, the earnest money is property, the value of that property would be a debit on the seller's statement, as it would reduce the amount of cash paid to the seller.

The amount of any new loan obtained from a lender is a credit to the buyer (as it is paid into his closing account) and does not appear on the seller's statement.

The amount of any financing provided by the seller, whether in the form of a purchase money mortgage or a contract for deed, and the amount of any loan or other encumbrances (unpaid taxes, special assessments, deeds of trust, etc.) assumed by the buyer are credits to the buyer and debits to the seller.

Any encumbrances not assumed by the buyer that are paid off at closing by the seller would appear as debits to the seller.

The buyer may also have to pay for a home inspection and/or pest and dry rot inspection. Often, loan and inspection fees are paid for at the time of the inspection or the loan application. If not, the buyer is debited the cost at closing.

Another possible charge, which could be paid by either the buyer or the seller, is for a home warranty.

If the buyer assumes the seller's existing loan, he would be credited the amount of the loan balance being assumed and be credited for unpaid interest from the date of the last payment. He would be debited the cost of an assumption fee charged by the lender for processing the paperwork.

Loan-Related Items

In general, items payable in connection with a loan (the fees lenders charge to process, approve and make the mortgage loan) are debits to the buyer, adding to the cost of acquiring the property. These items are neither credits nor debits to the seller.

Items related to a new loan include:

- a loan origination fee to cover the lender's administrative costs in processing the loan.
- an appraisal fee to pay for a statement of property value for the lender made by an independent appraiser.
- a credit report fee to cover the cost of a credit report.
- an inspection fee to cover inspections made by personnel of the lending institution or an outside inspector.
- a mortgage insurance premium to pay for mortgage insurance to protect the lender from loss due to payment default by the borrower.
- a hazard insurance premium to pay for property insurance to protect the buyer and lender against loss due to fire, windstorm, and other natural hazards. The buyer needs to pay at least the first year's premium at closing, and the lender will require the coverage to be for at least the full amount of the loan.
- a flood insurance premium to pay for flood insurance, if the property is within a special flood hazard area identified by FEMA.
- discount points as a one-time charge to adjust the lender's yield on the loan. This charge depends on how much the borrower wants to reduce the interest rate, as each point buys about a 1/8% reduction in the interest rate. Each point is equal to one percent of the mortgage amount.

If a lender charges four points on a $200,000 loan, this amounts to a charge of $8,000.
$200,000 x 4% = $8,000.

- interest accruing on the new loan from the date of settlement to the start of the period covered by the first monthly payment (normally the first day of the month following closing). If the closing is close to the end of the month, the lender may ask escrow to collect interest for the remainder of the month and the entire following month and then start the loan repayment period the month after that.

A closing takes place on April 16. The first monthly payment is due on June 1, including the interest charges for the month of May. At closing, the lender collects interest for the period from April 16 to May 1. In calculating the amount, the first step is to calculate the annual interest (by multiplying the loan balance by the interest rate). The second step is to multiply the answer by the number of days from closing to the end of the month of closing and then divide by 365. If the loan amount were $120,000 @ 6% interest, the buyer would be charged $295.89 ($120,000 x 6% x 15 ÷ 365).

If a sale closed April 29, the buyer could be charged interest on the loan for two days in April and the entire month of May. Then the first loan payment would be July 1, to cover the month of June.

- a reserves (or escrow or impound) deposit if the buyer is paying 1/12 of the estimated annual insurance premiums, property taxes, special assessments and homeowners' association assessments in his monthly mortgage payments. At closing, the borrower makes an initial deposit into the reserve account so that with the regular monthly deposits added, there is enough to pay the annual taxes, premiums, and assessments when due.
- a tax service fee for the cost of having a tax service company procure the city and county tax bills and special tax district improvement assessment bills each year for the lender and verify the taxing description with the loan identification.

Title Charges

At closing, there are also title charges covering a variety of services performed by title companies and others directly related to the transfer of the title (title examination, title search, document preparation), as well as fees for title insurance, legal charges and settlement fees (also called closing fees or escrow fees).

In some states, attorneys may be allowed to prepare a chain of title, in lieu of using a title insurance company.

In escrow states, as opposed to attorney states, the escrow fee is the fee charged by the escrow agent to have the legal documents prepared and recorded, to collect funds, and to then disburse them to the parties entitled to receive them. This fee is based on the dollar amount of the transaction, so the greater the transaction amount, the greater the fee.

Included in this fee may be the cost for reporting the transaction to the IRS on a 1099-S form. A real estate reporting entity (such as escrow) must file an information report (Form 1099-S), showing the sale price on a real estate sale or exchange, unless the transaction involves a principal residence with a sales price of $250,000 or less for an individual, or $500,000 or less for a married couple, and make sure a signed 1099 certificate is obtained from each person.

In transactions involving the sale of property by a nonresident alien, the **Foreign Investment in Real Property Tax Act** requires that the buyer withhold a tax of 10% of the gross proceeds, unless he uses the property as a residence and the purchase price is less than $300,000. For transactions involving a foreign seller, the listing agent should have the seller sign an affidavit stating that he is a resident alien, if this is the case, and have the affidavit furnished to the buyer.

In closings involving settlement meetings, there is no escrow fee, but there may be a number of additional separate charges for title search, document preparation, notary fee and attorney fees:

- A document preparation fee covers the cost of preparation of final legal papers, such as a mortgage, note or deed.
- A notary fee is charged for the cost of having a licensed person affix his name and seal to various documents authenticating the execution of these documents by the parties.
- Attorney fees may be charged for legal services provided to the lender in connection with the settlement.

An item that may be debited to both buyer and seller at closing is the cost of title insurance. In most areas, the buyer provides the lender with a lender's title policy. Custom in the area dictates whether the seller pays for the buyer's title insurance or not.

There are also government recording and transfer charges. Normally the buyer is responsible for paying fees for recording instruments pertaining to the ownership of the property, and the seller is responsible for fees for recording instruments to clear title.

In some states or localities a conveyance or excise tax is charged to the seller. The amount charged is a percentage of the sales price.

Commission

If there was a broker in a transaction, the seller usually pays the listing broker a sales commission. It is usually a percentage of the selling price of the property, negotiated between the seller and the broker. When several brokers work together to sell a property, the commission may be split among them, but the split may not be shown on the closing statement.

Legal Advice

If an attorney is called upon to provide advice or to draft a contract, the party represented by the attorney is debited the cost of the attorney unless there is an agreement otherwise.

Prorated Items

----- PRORATION -----

Certain expenses (and rental receipts) are prorated at the time of closing. Proration involves dividing or allocating an expense (or a sum of money received) proportionately between two parties based upon the relative time of use, interest or benefit enjoyed by each. In the context of real estate transactions, **proration** means to distribute or allocate  shares of ongoing income and expense items to the proper parties when the property changes ownership according to the contract or governing law. The purpose is to make certain the buyer and the seller each pay their fair share of expenses (i.e., the one who enjoyed the benefit of a service up to a specific date should pay the cost up to that date) or receive his fair share of receipts (usually rents).

Prorating is a process of determining who owes money, for what period and how much. Who owes money is easy to determine. If the seller has paid a bill in advance of the time it is due, the buyer will owe him money for the period after the closing date.

If the seller has paid to a date before the closing, or has not yet paid for items because the bill will not be due until after closing, he will credit the buyer with an amount to enable the buyer to pay the entire bill when it becomes due.

For income, the reverse is true. If the seller has received income covering a period that goes past the prorate date, he owes the buyer money to cover that unearned period. If he has not received income that was earned before the prorate date, the buyer owes him that money since the buyer will be receiving it after the closing.

The period for which the buyer owes money is the difference in time between the date to which the seller paid the item and the prorate date. The time for which the seller owes money is the difference between the prorate date and the date the bill is due.

Most commonly items are prorated to the closing date. It follows then that, the seller must pay any expenses accruing up to the day before closing and the buyer must pay expenses accruing on or after closing. Likewise, with respect to rents, the seller will receive that portion of rents attributable to the time up to the day before closing, and the buyer will receive the portion of rents attributable to the date of closing and thereafter. Prorations are generally required for property taxes, rents, ongoing association assessments, property and mortgage insurance, interest on loans, and water and sewer service charges.

Polly Gramm is selling her home to Al Packer, with the closing to occur on July 1. Property taxes for the year of closing are due on January 1 of the following year. The property taxes for the year must be allocated so that, at closing, Polly is charged for the property taxes attributable to January 1 through June 30 and Al is charged with the taxes for the remainder of the year.

In Arrears/In Advance

Expenses are either paid in arrears or in advance. If the payment is due at the end of the benefit period (i.e., after the benefit has been received), it is paid in *arrears* (e.g., mortgage interest. If the payment is due at the beginning of the benefit period (i.e., before the benefit has been received), it is made in *advance* (e.g., property insurance or monthly rent).

Accrued Expenses/Paid in Advance Expenses

Accrued expenses are items for which the seller owes a pro rata share as of the time of closing, but which are properly paid in arrears and are not due until after closing. Therefore, the buyer will eventually pay the full amount of the item, even though the payment partly covers a period for which the seller enjoyed the benefit of the item (e.g., unpaid real estate taxes, interest on a mortgage being assumed by the buyer, and unpaid association fees). When the buyer pays the full bill for the item in the future, his payment will partly cover a period of time the seller lived on the property. Therefore, at closing, the buyer is credited for the portion of expenses attributable to the seller (i.e., covering the time through the day before closing) and the seller is debited in the same amount.

Paid-in-advance expenses are items the seller paid in advance of closing for a period extending beyond the date of closing (e.g., prepaid real estate taxes, prepaid insurance premiums, prepaid utilities, and prepaid association fees). Because the buyer benefits from the amount prepaid by the seller to the extent it covers a period during which buyer will own the property at closing, the seller is credited for the portion of prepaid expenses covering the time from closing forward, and the buyer is debited in the same amount.

Reserve Accounts

Lenders may require or encourage **reserve** (or **escrow**) **accounts** for property taxes, hazard insurance, special assessments and/or homeowners' association assessments. When they are established, the borrower pays 1/12 of the estimated annual property taxes, hazard insurance premiums, special tax assessments and/or homeowners' assessments, along with the monthly principal and interest payments. This is held in a reserve (escrow) account, so there will be sufficient funds on hand to pay the full annual amount when due. The payments are referred to as reserve (or escrow or impound) payments. The items for which payments are made into a reserve account may also be known as **prepaids**.

Mel Lowe is purchasing a home with proceeds from a loan made by Left Bank. The annual property taxes on the property are $1,200. In addition to Mel's monthly principal and interest mortgage payment, Left Bank requires Mel to pay $100 into a reserve account each month, so the year's property taxes can be paid January 1 of the following year.

At closing the buyer will make an *initial* deposit into the reserve escrow account for any property taxes that have already accrued for the current tax year, so there will be enough in the account to pay the full year's tax bill when it becomes due. Additionally, for each prepaid item, the lender may require an additional deposit to provide a "buffer" of up to two months/payments, insuring that there will be sufficient funds on hand when the annual bill comes due, even if the last payment or two prior to the due date of the item are late.

Day of Closing

Most commonly the seller is considered to own the property through the day before the closing; the closing date is the buyer's first day of ownership. The buyer is considered the owner of the property *all day* on the day of closing, regardless of the actual time of day the closing occurs. Thus, generally, items are prorated to the closing date. The seller pays any expenses accrued to the closing date and the buyer pays expenses accruing on or after that date. For rents collected, the seller keeps the portion of rents collected for the current rent period to the day before closing and the buyer is credited for the portion of rents attributable to the closing date and thereafter.

With respect to a rental property, if a sale closes on October 19, the seller is liable for property expenses accruing and entitled to rents for the first 18 days of October. The buyer is responsible for expenses accruing and entitled to rents attributable as of October 19.

General Calculation of Prorations

Generally, all prorations are based on a 365-day year and/or the actual number of calendar days in a specific month.

The basic formula for prorating expenses paid in advance is shown below. To get the buyer's share of an expense paid in advance by the seller, the amount paid is either divided by the total number of days in the period to get a daily cost and then multiplied by the number of days used by the buyer or the amount paid is multiplied by the number of days used by the buyer and then divided by the total number of days in the period.

Total advance payment
by seller ($2,000) ÷
Total # of days in period (365) =
Daily cost of the item (5.479452)

Daily cost (5.479452) x
# of days used by buyer (35) =
Buyer's share of expense ($191.78)

$2,000 ÷365=5.479452
5.479452 x 35 = $191.78

OR

Total advance payment
by seller ($2,000) x
Actual # of days used by buyer (35)
Total # of days in period (365)
Buyer's share of expense ($191.78)

$2,000 x 35 ÷ 365 = $191.78

Debit the buyer and credit the seller that amount.

For Example

The seller prepays annual taxes of $3,650 on November 15. The sale closes on April 11 of the following year. Thus, the seller has paid the taxes for 81 days (20 days in April, 31 days in May, and 30 days in June) for which the buyer will enjoy possession of the property. $3,650 ÷ 365 days = $10/day. $10 x 81 days = $810. Debit the buyer $810, and credit the seller $810.

Conversely, to arrive at the seller's share of an expense paid in arrears by the buyer, the total arrears payment can be either divided by the total number of days in the period to get the daily cost and then multiplied by the number of days the seller benefited to get his share of the expense, or it can be multiplied by the seller's use and then divided by the total days in the period.

Total arrears payment
by buyer ($3,500) ÷
Total # of days in period (365) =
Daily cost of the item (9.589041)

Daily cost (9.589041) x
# of days used by buyer (56)
Seller's share of expense ($536.98)

$3,500 ÷ 365 = 9.589041
9.589041 x 56 = $536.98

OR

Total arrears payment
by buyer ($3,500) x
Actual # of days used by seller (56) ÷
Total # of days in period (365)
= Seller's share of expense ($536.98)

$3,500 x 56 ÷ 365 = $536.98

Debit the seller and credit the buyer that amount.

A transaction closes on August 1. Annual property taxes for the year of closing are $3,650, to be paid by buyer. The seller enjoys 31 days of ownership of the property in the tax year (from July 1), and the buyer enjoys ownership the remaining 334 days of the year. $3,650 ÷ 365 days = $10/day. $10 x 31 days = $310. Debit the seller $310 and credit the buyer $310.

When counting the number of days involved in prorations, be aware that the:
- beginning date is the first day of the period covered by the payment.
- ending date is the last day of the period covered by the payment.
- closing date is the buyer's first day of ownership.

In a proration the number of days counted for the seller and the buyer is the same. If the item being prorated has been paid by the seller prior to closing (e.g., the buyer is assuming the seller's hazard insurance policy), the seller is entitled to a refund based on the number of days from the day of closing through the ending date (i.e., the last day of the policy). If the item to be prorated has *not* been paid by the seller prior to closing (e.g., water service is to be paid in arrears by the buyer), the seller must pay at closing his pro rata share based on the number of days from the beginning date through the day before closing.

Items Typically Prorated

Some items that are typically prorated are as follows:
- Real property taxes for current year
- Personal property taxes
- Interest on loan assumed by buyer
- Hazard insurance premiums (assumed by buyer)
- Buyer's interest on new loan (amount not covered by first installment)
- Seller's interest on old loan (amount not covered by final installment)
- Rental income

Real Property Tax Proration

In Oregon, property taxes become a lien on July 1; the tax year runs from July 1 through June 30. The tax bill is mailed out in October, and one-third of the tax is due by November 15. Additional one-third payments are due by February 15 and May 15. Since the tax becomes a lien on July 1 and the tax bill is not sent out until October, closings occurring in July, August, September and at least the early part of October, will have taxes prorated based on the previous year's tax bill. When the closing occurs before the tax is paid, the prorated taxes will be a debit to the seller and a credit to the buyer, with the amount being determined by multiplying the daily amount of the tax by the number of days from July 1 through either the day before or the day of closing, depending on the agreement of the buyer and seller.

The formula for calculating the property tax proration is as follows:

> If the seller has not paid his taxes, multiply the annual tax by the number of days in the current tax year *before* the closing date and divide by the number of days in the tax year (365 days, or 366 days in a leap year).

For Example

The closing occurred on July 31, in a non-leap year. Taxes for the previous year were $2,000. The seller's share of taxes would be:

$2,000 x 30 days ÷ 365 days = $164.38 (seller's pro rata share)

Debit the seller (reducing his proceeds, because he is being relieved of the obligation to pay for a benefit he has already received). Credit the buyer (reducing the amount of cash he needs to pay at closing, because he is undertaking the obligation to pay in the future for a benefit the seller has already received).

For Example

The closing date is September 29, with the buyer responsible for the day of closing. Taxes last year were $1,095. Step one: determine who owes money. Since the tax bill has not been sent out, the seller owes the money for the period of July 1 through the day before closing, September 28 (since the buyer is responsible for September 29). Therefore, the tax is a debit to him and a credit to the buyer. Based on the actual number of days, the seller owes for 90 days (31 days in July, 31 days in August and 28 days in September). He owes the buyer $270 (90/365 of $1,095. The exact amount is obtained by multiplying 90 x 1,095 and dividing by 365).

> If the seller has paid his taxes, multiply the annual tax by the number of days remaining in the current tax year, being sure to include the day of closing and divide by the number of days in the tax year (365 days, or 366 days in a leap year).

For Example

The seller paid the annual tax bill of $2,190 in November. The sale closes February 15 of the following year (with the buyer responsible for the day of closing). Since the seller has paid to the end of the tax year, the buyer will reimburse him for the period from February 15 through June 30. This is a seller credit and a buyer debit. The buyer will owe the seller for 136 days (14 days in February [subtract the first 14 days of the month for which the seller is responsible from 28 days], plus 31 days for March, 30 for April, 31 for May and 30 for June). Multiply 1,095 by 136 and divide by 365 to calculate the exact amount. He owes $816. By paying all of his taxes for the year on November 15, the seller gets a 3% discount. However, when taxes are prorated, the tax owed ($2,190), not the discounted amount actually paid, is prorated.

Interest on Loan Assumed

This item is relevant if the buyer assumes the seller's current loan. It involves the interest accruing on the seller's current loan from the due date of the seller's last (final) payment up to the day before closing. The information necessary to calculate interest on the loan assumed is provided in the lender's loan assumption statement, which must be requested from that lender. If the buyer assumes the seller's existing loan and interest on the loan is charged *in arrears*, interest due on the loan from the due date of the seller's last (final) payment to the day before closing should be a seller debit and a buyer credit. This is because when the buyer makes the first installment payment after closing, it will include interest for the previous month, and he will be paying interest for a period during which the seller enjoyed use of the property (i.e., from the due date of seller's last payment to the day before closing).

The formula for prorating this item is as follows:

Unpaid principal balance at closing x interest rate = annual interest
Annual interest x actual number of days in the closing month through the day before closing ÷ 365 = interest on the loan assumed (i.e., the seller's share of interest for that month)

Debit the seller and credit the buyer.

For Example

An earnest money agreement calls for the buyer to assume a 9% loan with a $180,000 balance owed at the time of closing. Loan payments are due on the 1st of each month. The closing date is January 12, with interest prorated through January 11. At closing, the seller must give the buyer enough money to pay for 11 days interest on the $180,000. $180,000 x 9% x 11 ÷ 365 = $488.22. This is the amount the seller is debited and the buyer is credited for interest for the month.

For Example

Interest for a monthly amortized loan with a current unpaid principal balance of $187,650 at 5.5% interest paid in arrears, closing on August 10, with payments due the first of each month and the seller's last payment made on August 1, is as follows:

$187,650 x 5.5% = $10,320.75 per year (annual interest) x 9 days ÷ 365 days = $254.48

This is the amount the seller is debited and the buyer is credited for interest for the month.

In this way, the buyer will not be penalized when making the September 1 payment, including interest in arrears for the entire month of August, because the buyer will have been compensated at closing for the seller's nine days of interest responsibility.

Seller's Interest on Old Loan (Amount not Covered by Final Installment)

This item also relates to the interest owed by the seller on his existing loan, except the loan is being paid off rather than assumed by buyer. Since the buyer will not pay for the day of closing, the seller must pay for that day.

A seller has a current loan that will be paid off at closing. His payments are due the first of the month. He timely made his August 1 payment. Closing is set for August 10. The closer will count the number of days from (and including) the seller's last due date through the day of closing. Thus, the seller will owe interest for 10 days.

Sometimes this interest is referred to as **accrued interest** or unpaid interest. The formula for determining this amount is as follows:

Principal balance (as of last payment before closing) x annual % rate = annual interest
Annual interest x number of days from final payment to closing ÷ 365 = unpaid interest/interest owed

Payments are due on the first day of each month and are current. The loan balance is $192,000, the interest rate is 10%, and closing is May 19. Solution:

$192,000 x 10 % = $19,200 (annual interest) x 19 days ÷ 365 = $999.45 (unpaid interest/interest owed)

This amount will be debited the seller.

If payments were due on a day other than the first, e.g., the 20th of each month, and closing is August 15, the seller would owe interest for the period of July 20 through 31 and the first 15 days of August. He would owe for 12 days in July (31 minus 19) and 15 days in August for a total of 27 days.

Payments are due on the fifteenth day of each month and payments are current. The loan balance is $154,700 at 7% interest. Closing is September 6.

August	17 days (31 days minus 14 days)
September	6 days
Total	23 days

$154,700 x 7 % x 23 days ÷ 365 = $682.38 (unpaid interest/interest owed)

Interest on New Loan (aka Prepaid Interest)

With most home loans, interest is paid in arrears (i.e., each monthly payment pays interest for the preceding month) rather than in advance (i.e., paying interest for the

month that follows). Even so, the *initial installment* of a home payment usually creates a unique situation, requiring the buyer/borrower to pay a small amount of interest in advance.

When the buyer obtains a new loan, he will be responsible for paying interest as of the day of closing until the end of that month. His first loan payment will cover the first full month after closing. Each installment payment will include interest for the *month prior* to the payment. If a transaction closed on March 15, the first installment will be due on May 1. The first payment will include interest for all of April, but not interest for the final days of March. Since the interest for these 17 days (31 days in March minus the 14 days prior to closing) will not be covered by the buyer's initial installment, it must be paid in advance, in a lump sum at closing. The buyer will be debited this amount. Thereafter, all interest will be paid in arrears.

Note: In calculating the prorate, the number of days in the month before closing are subtracted from the total number of days in the month.

Interest on a new loan is calculated as follows:

> Total loan amount x interest rate = annual interest
> Annual interest x number of days remaining in month (including day of closing) ÷ 365 = total interest owed

For Example

The loan is $205,000. The interest rate is 6.5%. There are 16 days of interest not covered by the first installment payment. The amount of interest on the new loan is calculated as follows:

$205,000 x 6.5% x 16 days ÷ 365 days = $584.11

For Example

An earnest money agreement calls for the buyer to obtain a 9%, $100,000 loan. Loan payments will be due on the 1st of each month. The closing date is January 17. For new loans, at closing the buyer is charged interest from the day of closing to the end of the month. This interest is a debit to the buyer. To calculate the number of days, subtract 16 (the number of days in January for which the buyer does not owe interest) from 31. The buyer owes interest for 15 days. At closing, he must give the lender enough money to pay 15 days interest on the $100,000. $100,000 x 9% x 15 ÷ 365 = $369.86, the amount the buyer is debited for interest on the new loan.

Rental Income Proration

Normally the owner of rental property will collect rent in advance for the upcoming month. In a closing involving a rental property those rents will be prorated. Generally, the owner is entitled to rent amounts attributable to the period up to the day before closing and the buyer is entitled to amounts attributable to the period from closing forward.

The formula for prorating monthly rent when rent is collected in advance is as follows:

Monthly rent ÷ number of days in the *month at issue = daily rent
Daily rent x number of days the buyer owns the property = buyer's pro rata share

*If rent is not due on the first of the month, then count the number of days covered by
 the particular rent payment.

For Example

The property is a single rental unit. Rent is $800, due on the 5th day of each month. The
closing is October 24. October rent was paid on time (eliminating rents collected versus
accrued issues). The rent payment made to the seller on October 5 is for the period ending
November 4. The buyer is entitled to rents attributable to October 24 (the closing date)
and thereafter. So, the seller owes the buyer for 12 days of rent (8 days in October and 4
days in November).

Solution:

October	8 days (31 days – 23 days)
November	4 days
Total	12 days

$800 ÷ 31 days = $25.806451 (daily rent)
$25.806451 x 12 = $309.68 (the buyer's pro rata share of rents)

The Bottom Line

----- BUYER'S AND SELLER'S CHECKS -----

When all of the buyer's credits have been subtracted from his debits, the result is the amount of cash the buyer needs to close. This is normally covered by a wire transfer to the buyer's escrow account or by a cashier's check paid at closing. This check is a credit to the buyer. When it is added to the other credits, the total of the buyer's credits will equal the buyer's debits.

When the seller's debits have been subtracted from his credits, the result is the check the seller will receive from closing. This check is a debit to the seller. When it is added to the other debits, the total of the seller's debits will equal his credits.

----- IN AND OUT -----

One way to help keep credits and debits straight is to consider that the closing agent is preparing the closing statement; it reflects his vision of the transaction. Any money he collects for a party is a credit for that party. Any money he pays out is a debit. The money he collects has to equal the money he pays out so that he has nothing left when he is done.

The Buyer

Based on this thinking, money the buyer owes at closing, that the closing agent must pay *out*, make up the buyer's debits. This includes the following:

- Purchase price
- Closing costs (e.g., half the escrow fee and title insurance for the new loan lender)
- Loan fees for a new loan or an assumption fee for an assumed loan
- Reimbursement of seller prepaids

Money or credit put *into* the closing agent's buyer account to pay these constitutes the buyer's credits. This includes the following:

- Any financing, whether a new loan, assumed loan or seller financing (purchase money mortgage or land sales contract)
- Any money given by the buyer (such as earnest money or a check for the balance owed at closing)
- Any prorated amounts credited by the seller (such as for prepaid rents or unpaid taxes)

Buyer Credits (paid **into** his account)	Buyer Debits (paid **out of** his account)
• Earnest money • Assumptions of existing encumbrances • New loans • Prepaid items received by seller • Check he pays at closing	• Purchase price • Reserve account • Property insurance • Recording fees • Legal fees and escrow fees • Prorated share of property taxes paid in advance by seller • Mortgagee's title policy (for new loan) • Loan origination fee, appraisal fee, credit report, tax registration, mortgage insurance, staking or survey • Assumption fee • Interest adjustment charges • Judgments • Personal property not included in sales price

The Seller

Money or credit put *into* the closing agent's seller account constitutes the seller's credits. This is the money the buyer is to pay the seller on the day of closing, typically just:

- the purchase price; and
- reimbursement for prepaid taxes.

Money the closing agent must pay *out* makes up the seller's debits. This includes the following:

- The amount of any existing loan, and the interest accrued on that loan since the last payment, whether the loan is assumed by the buyer or paid off at closing
- The amount of any new loan the seller gives the buyer, whether in the form of a purchase money mortgage loan or land sales contract
- Closing costs (e.g., half the escrow fee and title insurance for the buyer)
- Prorated share of unpaid taxes
- Broker commission
- Check to seller

> **NOTE:** Any check written by the closing agent is a debit (e.g., the check to the principal broker or to the seller), as it comes out of a closing account. Any check written by someone other than the closing agent (e.g., the buyer's earnest money and his check to close) is a credit, as it goes into a closing account.

Seller Credits (paid **into** his account)	Seller Debits (paid **out of** his account)
• Selling price • Prorations of taxes paid in advance • Insurance premiums refunded • Rent not yet collected • Refund of interest paid in advance • Refund of reserves • Personal property added to sales price	• Owner's title policy • Commission (unless a note or property) • Recording satisfaction of liens • Legal fees and escrow fees • Discount points paid for buyer • Judgments • Purchase money mortgage or contract • Termite inspection/treatment • Survey • Excise tax • Rents collected in advance, security deposits, last month's rent • Obligations owed • Existing loan • Unpaid interest, taxes • Loan prepayment penalty • Amount seller will receive from closing

Records

Maintenance of adequate records is an important part of a broker's risk management program, as these records may provide him with documentation sufficient to counter claims that his actions or the actions of associated licensees were incompetent, negligent or fraudulent.

----- REQUIRED RECORDS -----

Agency rules provide that a broker's records of professional real estate activity must include complete, legible and permanent copies of all documents required by law or voluntarily generated during a real estate transaction, including offers whether accepted or closed, by or through brokers to clients.

Required records include the following:
- A copy of any written agreement creating an agency relationship with a client, signed by all of the parties to the agreement (This would include a listing agreement, a buyer agency agreement, and a property management agreement.)
- A copy of any written acknowledgment of an agency relationship with a client, signed by all of the parties to the acknowledgment (This would include the sale agreement that has the acknowledgment of the agency relationship in it, or a separate agency acknowledgment if it is not included in the sale agreement.)
- A copy of any written agreement for the listing, sale, purchase, rental, lease, lease-option or exchange of real property generated by a broker while engaging in professional real estate activity, signed by all of the parties to the agreement
- A copy of any other written document falling within the scope of the agency relationship provided to or received by a client through a broker during the term of an agency relationship
- A copy of any closing statement showing all receipts, disbursements and adjustments, and signed by the seller(s) and the buyer(s), for any transaction in which a principal broker performed the closing
- A copy of any receipt issued by a licensee to evidence acceptance of funds or documents
- A copy of any vouchers or bills or obligations paid by the principal broker for the account of a client or customer
- All other required financial records:
  - These include:
    - a complete ledger account and record of all funds received in the broker's professional real estate activity showing from whom the funds were received, the date of the receipt, the place and date of deposit and when the transaction was completed or the offer failed, the final disposition of the funds, promissory notes, or other consideration.
    - all checks, including voided checks.

- a record of the transfer of promissory notes and other forms of consideration by a ledger account or by other means, such as written proof of transmittal or receipt.
- a record of the transfer of other documents by written proof of transmittal or receipt, maintained in the broker's offer or transaction file.
- copies of any checks received, and a dated, acknowledged receipt for any check returned to the offeror.
- for every deposit made into a trust account, a deposit slip identifying the offer or transaction to which the deposit pertains, in the form of a written notation of the file number assigned to the offer/transaction.
- bank statements and dated and signed monthly reconciliations for each client's trust account, filed in logical sequence.

A copy of every listing agreement, earnest money receipt, addendum and counteroffer must be reviewed, initialed, and dated by the branch manager or principal broker within seven business days after is it accepted, rejected or withdrawn, and then maintained in the broker's office. A written record of the date and time of the tender of each offer or counteroffer must be maintained in the offer or transaction file, along with a written record of the offeree's response to the offer.

----- FILES -----

A principal broker's files will include the following:
- Listing files
- Buyer agency files
- Transaction files
- Files for offers, whether accepted or closed

Listing File
The Real Estate Agency recommends that the following items be kept in a broker's **listing file**.

The Listing
There should be a completed copy of the listing agreement, signed by all of the owner(s), with a termination date, authorizations for entry to the MLS and for placement of a For Sale sign on the property, and specific authorization for any types of advertising or promotion of the property that might be intrusive.

In reviewing the agreement, the principal broker should make sure that it is signed by all of the sellers who are to be selling the property. He must ensure there is evidence of ownership or of the right to sign the listing for the seller. If the listing is not signed by the owner of record, the file needs documentation showing the authority of the person signing to sign on behalf of the owner.

Agency Disclosure

Most brokers will require evidence that the Oregon Real Estate Agency Disclosure pamphlet was given to the seller. Generally the evidence is a signed copy of the Disclosed Limited Agency Agreement, in which the seller acknowledges receipt of the pamphlet. If there is no Disclosed Limited Agency Agreement, a signed copy of the pamphlet should be placed in the file. If the seller refuses to sign a copy, the listing licensee should make a written note of the time and date of presentation, cite the seller's refusal, and place the note in the listing file.

Property Information

The file should contain:

- a completed and signed copy of a seller's property disclosure statement for a residential property transaction.
- the source of the measurements used in the listing, such as the tax assessor's records, a recent real estate appraisal report, or a copy of a recorded plat or a description taken from a recorded document.
- verification of building and lot sizes and what source was used to provide that information.
- any specific information about the property, such as CC&Rs, owner association bylaws, special assessments pending, planned road construction, a copy of the preliminary title report, and documentation relating to land use restrictions and zoning.
- information about any tenant and the terms of the lease or rental agreement.

Documentation of Agent's Efforts

The file should have documentation showing:

- how the listing price was established, such as a competitive market analysis, an appraisal report, the tax-assessed valuation or the owner's opinion.
- marketing activity, including, media advertising, evidenced by a copy of the ad content or publication/broadcast information; the MLS information sheet; flyers and brochures produced and used; MLS tour information; and open house activity.
- listing modifications, such as signed extensions, price changes, and changes in disclosures, and their basis.
- any written estimates of seller's net proceeds provided to the seller.
- the licensee's notes or diary entries.
- all correspondence, including faxes and printouts of e-mail.
- any promises, pledges of service, or other agreements made by the listing agent to obtain the listing, such as promises to hold open houses or advertise on the Internet.
- the principal broker's dated initials on any document of agreement.

Buyer Agency File

The Real Estate Agency recommends that the following items be kept in a **buyer agency file**:

- A signed buyer agency agreement, if one exists
- A signed Disclosed Limited Agency Agreement, or if there is no Disclosed Limited Agency Agreement, a signed copy of the agency disclosure pamphlet
- Documentation, in the form of notes of discussions or in the form of an activity list, of what the buyer has told him in terms of wants and needs, including such nonmaterial factors of concern as an aversion to any property in which there has been a death, or a violent death
- The buyer's financial qualifications and any prequalification or preapproval letters
- Any pledges or promises of service made by the broker to induce the buyer to sign the buyer's agency agreement
- A record of the real estate shown by the broker to the buyer
- The principal broker's dated initials showing his review and approval of the documents

Transaction File

If there is an accepted offer for the client, the broker will normally set up a **transaction file**. The file should be assigned a consecutive, sequential transaction number as soon as there is an accepted offer or counteroffer from a client in the transaction. Transaction numbers may be in any logical sequence, such as numerical or alphabetical.

The following are recommended by the Agency to be kept in the transaction file:

- The full names and addresses of the buyers or sellers or other parties with telephone, e-mail, fax, and other means of contact
- Copies of the complete, signed agreement between the parties, and any counteroffer, acknowledgment, addendum, or other document that is part of the initial agreement or that confirms that contingencies have been satisfied or removed in the transaction
- A full legal description of the property
- A record (by diary entry, memo, or other format) of who, how, and when the offer was delivered and presented and any counteroffers, and documentation of any representations by licensees or principals made as part of the offer
- For residential property, a copy of the seller's property disclosure statement, acknowledged
- A copy of the earnest money note, cash, check, or car title document, and indication of the disposition of the deposit
- Verification of land use, zoning, and any specialized limits on use of the property, such as flood plain restrictions and natural resource overlay zoning and restrictions
- Evidence of all work for clients

- The preliminary title report, with a record of review and discussion of any problems with the client
- Documentation of all disclosures and recommendations made to the client
- Copies of all correspondence, including faxes, to or from the client, the unrepresented party, other licensees or authorized representatives
- Diary notes
- If escrow closed, a copy of the client's closing statement to show the successful closing and disbursement of the broker's earned commission
- If the principal broker closed, a complete record of money received and disbursed, copies of all closing documents and an explanation of any problems arising in closing and how the problems were resolved
- If an associate closed, a copy of the required written authorization
- If the sale fails, any information on the reason and the disposition of the earnest money
- The principal broker's dated initials on all documents of agreement

File for an Unaccepted Offer or Counteroffer

When an offer or counteroffer is not accepted, a consecutively numbered transaction file is not required. However, most brokers will keep the offer or counteroffer with the related listings or buyer's agency agreements to show what they had done for the client. The following records are recommended by the Agency to be kept for an unaccepted offer or counteroffer:

- A complete, signed copy of the unaccepted offer, rejection or counteroffer, including the dated, timed signatures and initials on the documents
- Notation of the delivery of the Agency Disclosure pamphlet to the client, and the final agency acknowledgment of both parties
- A copy of the earnest money tendered with the offer or counteroffer, and documentation of the return of the deposit to the offeror upon rejection of the offer or counteroffer
- The principal broker's dated initials on all documents of agreement and documenting rejection or an unaccepted counteroffer
- Copies of any competitive market analyses or letter opinions prepared for the buyer or the seller
- The Loan Estimate of the buyer's down payment and closing costs or the seller's net proceeds
- Evidence of all disclosures and recommendations the parties followed or chose not to follow
- Copies of all correspondence, including faxes
- The licensee's diary notes and other notes of conversations

A principal broker must maintain and store complete and accurate records of professional real estate activity, including any items generated through e-mail or other electronic means, for a period of six years following the date of the creation of the record. Records of each transaction shall be maintained for a period of not less than six years after the date the transaction closed or failed. Under written company policy, brokers associated with a principal broker may maintain and store records of professional real estate activity at the main office of the principal broker, and records of professional real estate activity originating at a branch office may be maintained and stored at either that branch office or at the main office of the principal broker.

A principal broker must maintain at his office a means of viewing copies of documents or records. He must provide, at his expense, a paper copy of any document or record requested by the Agency.

If a principal broker closes his office, he must not only release all of the licenses of the persons under his supervision, but he must also arrange to maintain all required records within the State of Oregon.

A principal broker may store records of professional real estate activity in a single location in Oregon other than his office, the main office of the principal broker or a branch office, so long as the records are readily available at that location for inspection, if he first:

- notifies the Commissioner in writing of the intended removal of records. This notice must include the address of the new location for the records.
- gives written authorization to the Commissioner to inspect the records at the new location. This authorization must include the name of any necessary contact and the means of gaining access to the records for an inspection. The principal broker must notify the Commissioner of any change in the contact or means of access within ten days after the change occurs.

Electronic Image Storage Media

A principal broker or property manager may use **electronic image storage** media to retain and store copies of all listings, deposit receipts, canceled checks, client trust account records and other documents executed by him or obtained by him in connection with any professional real estate activity transaction, when the following requirements are satisfied:

- The electronic image storage must be nonerasable "write once, read many" (WORM) and must not allow changes to the stored document or record.
- The stored document or record is made or preserved as part of and in the regular course of business.
- The original record from which the stored document or record was copied was made or prepared by the principal broker or property manager or his employees at or near the time of the act, condition or event reflected in the record.

- The custodian of the record is able to identify the stored document or record, the mode of its preparation, and the mode of storing it on the electronic image storage.
- The electronic image storage media must contain a reliable indexing system that provides ready access to a desired document or record, appropriate quality control of the storage process to ensure the quality of imaged documents or records, and date ordered arrangement of stored documents or records to ensure a consistent and logical flow of paperwork to preclude unnecessary search time.
- At least once each month, the principal broker must back up any data stored in the computerized system necessary to produce the records. The back-up data must be retained for no less than 60 days and made available to the Commissioner or to the Commissioner's authorized representatives on demand.

----- TECHNOLOGY IN REAL ESTATE SALES -----

The world is changing fast and real estate sales is now heavily into technology. More and more licensees are completing real estate transactions using electronic signatures. Many of these licensees are finding that they can work faster and smarter by not having to drive all over town for signatures or wait for that really bad Fax copy of a signature to come in. While most documents today are emailed instead of mailed or faxed there are concerns. Licensees still have to do the same things such as provide copies of signed documents to all parties, regardless if it is an electronic or pen and ink signature. All these documents must be reviewed by a principal broker. There are many transactions today that are being completed and closed with little or even no actual paperwork. Electronic signatures on both ends, principal broker review electronically with an electronic record of the review, and paperwork including home inspections etc. arriving at escrow only in electronic media. The principal broker needs to make sure that these transactions are not being accomplished by eliminating required steps in the process. The real estate agency has already written rules specific to electronic advertising and specifies that document review and storage can be accomplished electronically…with stipulations.

Brain Teaser

Reinforce your understanding of the material by correctly completing the following sentences:

1. If a principal broker conducts a closing, he must ensure that the buyer and the seller each receive a complete detailed closing statement showing the amount and purpose of all receipts, adjustments and _____.

2. Earnest money is a buyer's _____.

3. When the closing occurs before the tax is paid, the prorated taxes will be a _____ to the seller and a _____ to the buyer.

4. A _____ file should be assigned a consecutive, sequential transaction number as soon as there is an offer or counteroffer from a client in the transaction.

5. Records of professional real estate activity originating at a _____ office may be maintained and stored at either that branch office or at the main office of the principal broker.

Brain Teaser Answers

1. If a principal broker conducts a closing, he must ensure that the buyer and the seller each receive a complete detailed closing statement showing the amount and purpose of all receipts, adjustments and **disbursements**.

2. Earnest money is a buyer's **credit**.

3. When the closing occurs before the tax is paid, the prorated taxes will be a **debit** to the seller and a **credit** to the buyer.

4. A **transaction** file should be assigned a consecutive, sequential transaction number as soon as there is an offer or counteroffer from a client in the transaction.

5. Records of professional real estate activity originating at a **branch** office may be maintained and stored at either that branch office or at the main office of the principal broker.

Review – Oregon Closings and Records

This lesson covers calculations involved in preparing a closing statement and broker recordkeeping requirements.

Broker Closings

Administrative rules require that the listing broker promptly close the transaction, unless all parties to the transaction agree in writing to delegate the closing function to someone else, such as an escrow agent, an attorney, or another broker engaged in the transaction. A real estate broker may act as an escrow agent without obtaining an escrow agent license when he performs the closing for the principals in a transaction in which he participated as a broker, and the principals are not charged a separate fee for the escrow services.

In Oregon, an escrow agent may accept funds into escrow only with dated written instructions, or a dated written agreement between the parties, with or without the services of a real estate licensee. Escrow may then review legal documents for accuracy and typographical errors and may disburse funds as authorized by both principals. They cannot, however, draft legal documents or perform a legal review of them.

A principal broker can delegate the function to a licensee associated with him. To do so, he must provide written authorization to handle the closing function, file a copy with the Commissioner, and directly supervise the closing.

Credits and Debits

On a closing statement, the buyer's charges, or debits, are all amounts due and payable at the time of closing, to the seller and others. They are amounts he owes the seller and amounts to pay closing and loan costs (but not the loan itself), on the day of closing. The buyer's credits are what he uses to pay his debits.

The seller's credits are amounts the buyer owes him on the day of closing. This is typically just the sales price and reimbursement of prepaid taxes. His debits reflect how his credits are disbursed on the day of closing. These include the amount of any financing with which he is involved, closing costs, amounts he owes the buyer, and the check for the sales proceeds. The final debit for the seller is the amount he will actually receive from the closing.

Prorates

In Oregon, property taxes become a lien on July 1, and the tax year runs from July 1 through June 30. The formula for calculating the property tax proration is as follows: If the seller has not paid his taxes, multiply the annual tax by the number of days in the current tax year *before* the closing date and divide by the number of days in the tax year (365 days, or 366 days in a leap year). If the seller has paid his taxes, multiply the annual tax by the number of days remaining in the current tax year, being sure to include the day of closing and divide by the number of days in the tax year (365 days, or 366 days in a leap year).

The formula for prorating interest on an existing loan being assumed is as follows: Unpaid principal balance at closing x interest rate = annual interest. Annual interest x actual number of days in the closing month through the day before closing ÷ 365 = interest on the loan assumed (i.e., the seller's share of interest for that month). Debit the seller and credit the buyer.

Interest on a new loan is calculated as follows: Total loan amount x interest rate = annual interest. Annual interest x number of days remaining in month (including day of closing) ÷ 365 = total interest owed.

One way to help keep credits and debits straight is to consider that the closing agent is preparing the closing statement; it reflects his vision of the transaction. Any money he collects for a party is a credit for that party. Any money he pays out is a debit. The money he collects has to equal the money he pays out, so he has nothing left when he is done. Based on this thinking, money the buyer owes at closing, that the closing agent must pay *out*, make up the buyer's debits. Money or credit put *into* the closing agent's buyer account to pay these constitutes the buyer's credits.

Money or credit put *into* the closing agent's seller account constitutes the seller's credits. Money the closing agent must pay *out* makes up the seller's debits.

Records Retention

A copy of every listing agreement, earnest money receipt, addendum and counteroffer must be reviewed, initialed, and dated by the branch manager or principal broker within seven business or banking days after is it accepted, rejected or withdrawn, and maintained in the broker's office. A broker must maintain and store complete and accurate records of professional real estate activity for a period of six years following the date of the creation of the record. Records of each transaction must be maintained for a period of not less than six years after the date the transaction closed or failed. A principal broker who closes his office must release all of the licenses of the persons under his supervision and arrange to maintain all required records within the State of Oregon.

A broker may store records of professional real estate activity in a single location in Oregon other than his office, the main office of the principal broker or a branch office, so long as the records are readily available for inspection at that location and if he first notifies the Commissioner in writing and gives written authorization to the Commissioner to inspect the records at the new location within ten days after the change occurs.

A real estate broker or property manager may use electronic image storage media to retain and store copies of all listings, deposit receipts, canceled checks, client trust account records and other documents executed by him or obtained by him in connection with any professional real estate activity transaction.

Oregon Manuals and Reports

Overview

This lesson covers policies and procedures manuals and financial reports. The advantages and format of a good company policies and procedures manual are covered. An explanation of two key financial reports (the balance sheet and the income statements) and federal and state tax requirements conclude the lesson.

Objectives

Upon completion of this lesson, the student should be able to:

1. Explain the supervisory role of a principal broker.
2. Identify the elements of a policies and procedures manual.
3. Describe the use of the manual in training and in setting out grievance procedures.
4. Discuss options for policies relating to personal transactions of associates.
5. Describe the contents of a balance sheet.
6. Describe the contents of an income statement.
7. Describe the various taxes and payroll reports for which a principal broker may be liable as an employer.

Content and Purpose of a Policy Manual

----- POLICIES AND PROCEDURES MANUAL -----

Because of the independent contractor relationship and the responsibility to train and supervise affiliated licensees, the brokerage business has its challenges with regard to supervision of the affiliated licensees. Despite the relative freedom licensed associates do have, the principal broker must exercise proper management control and techniques to ensure compliance with basic standards of competence, ethical behavior, and the law.

Proper management starts with the principal broker's associates having a clear understanding of the type of performance expected of them and the degree of supervision and assistance they can expect from the principal broker.

In order to create this understanding, the principal broker should make sure that the independent contractor agreement clearly defines the responsibilities of the parties. He should also have a policies and procedures manual to guide the licensed associates in their performance so they act in accordance with the goals and objectives of the firm. The manual is not a contract. The independent contractor agreement may be attached to the manual or referenced in the manual, but it should not be included in the manual itself.

Policies and Procedures

Policies and procedures are standing plans for repetitive action. They are available to cover certain situations whenever they arise.

A **policy** is a general guide to action. It serves as a control device to influence behavior. It does not provide instruction in how to perform specific tasks. Policies will help establish the philosophy that management wants to instill in an organization.

"It is our policy to encourage dress in a businesslike fashion. You only have one opportunity to create a good impression."

"The broker always adheres to all federal, state and local laws and regulations whereby any person, regardless of race, creed, color, religion, national origin, sex, marital status, familial status, source of income, handicap, or sexual orientation, has the right to choose where he wishes to live and the homeowner will agree to sell his home to them, if all preset conditions are met."

"You are required to follow the state license law to the letter."

"Personal or business problems of clients are to be kept strictly confidential and should not be discussed with others."

"You must not give legal advice, directly or indirectly."

"ABC Realty requires the taking of exclusive listings for a 180 day period at 7% commission. New home sales, builder and developer activity, and condominium developments are normally at 6% commission. Commissions and time periods can be negotiated for higher-priced properties."

These are policies, as they are general guidelines for actions and do not instruct the licensee in how to:
- dress.
- handle situations in which he may be asked to violate fair housing laws.
- respond to requests for legal advice.
- get a listing.

Procedures are specific statements as to what actions are to be taken. These would be intended to more rigidly control behavior. They would provide guidance as to how to dress, handle uncomfortable situations, respond to requests for legal advice, etc.

A procedure is a standard method of operation, indicating the preferred method of handling the described situation rather than the only method. It serves as a guideline that can be referenced at any time for consistency in performing tasks.

Particularly in real estate brokerage, where the associates are independent contractors rather than employees, these procedures would be limited to activities dictated by legislative and common law obligations of the principal broker for supervision of the associates, as well as the need to provide order in an environment in which large numbers of people must work together. This would include procedures for such items as handling earnest money deposits, ordering lockboxes, taking signs from the office and returning them, use of the phones, methods of completing and turning in contracts, and providing agency disclosures.

Purpose of a Policy Manual

The **policy manual** is a statement or declaration of the company's policy, philosophy, procedures, and rules and regulations. It will generally spell out what is expected of an associate in his day-to-day activities, as well as what the associate can expect of the company.

The standard operating procedures should provide answers to routine questions on practices and procedures, giving associates standards to follow each time a particular situation arises.

Because it is impossible to cover every contingency, the manual should be kept simple. Rather than attempt to cover procedures for every business situation or set broad policy limitations, the manual should focus on policies and procedures that enable associates to perform most activities with a minimal amount of supervision and considerable freedom of action.

The manual is best developed by members of the firm under the direction of an administrator. Members of the firm can be encouraged to participate in writing and interpreting policy and in making additions and changes to the manual.

Manual Contents

The manual should have a table of contents and/or index. It should include those items that will make it easier to delegate authority and responsibility and help establish the most economical and effective way of doing certain jobs.

One item the manual should contain is a written company policy that sets forth the types of relationships real estate licensees associated with the business may establish. Such a policy may include:

- provisions regarding how affiliated licensees will comply with the requirements for establishing agency relationships.
- procedures to ensure the protection of confidential information.
- provisions regarding the supervision and control of licensees associated with the business in the fulfillment of their duties and obligations to their respective clients.
- provisions regarding the supervision of licensed personal assistants employed by the brokerage or employed by licensees associated with the brokerage.

In addition to these items, many manuals will state the objectives of the company and the expected objectives of its associates. In stating the objectives, they may establish company goals as well as individual goals.

Objectives help provide a sound basis of control and coordination between branch offices and managers. They develop performance standards that may become an individual associate's guidelines for measuring his own performance. Only if associates and managers can see and fully understand the objectives can they accept and be fully committed to them.

Long-range objectives are the goals for several years in future. They may indicate:
- a desired expected share of the market.
- new services to be developed.
- the expected financial condition of the company.
- a means of improving community relations.

Short-term objectives are smaller steps to reach the long-range objectives. These might  include the opening of a branch office by a certain date, with the office having a certain number of associates and corresponding revenue within a certain period.

As a way in which to further explain the purpose and goals of the company, many principal brokers begin the manual with a statement of the company's history. Whatever the principal broker feels associates should know, information that will not change for a while and that is essential for an associate to operate in the company, should be included in the manual.

There are a myriad of topics that are often covered in an office policies and procedures manual, including the following:

General Office	Networking/Education
o Allocation of desk space o Closing office at night o Handling of lockbox & keys o Telephone procedures o Hours of operation o Holidays and office closures o Principal broker/manager availability	o Professional organizations o Education policies o Dues and fees

Sales Issues	Bookkeeping/Recordkeeping
<ul><li>Advertising procedures</li><li>Agency relationships</li><li>Agency duties</li><li>Associates buying and selling for own account</li><li>Commission controversies</li><li>Commission policies</li><li>Confidential information</li><li>Co-op sales and co-op situations with another broker who wants to show an associate's listings</li><li>Dispute resolution</li><li>Floor time policies</li><li>How associates should treat people who come into the office</li><li>Inspection tours</li><li>Intra-office or interoffice exchange of clients</li><li>Internet policies</li><li>Legal advice</li><li>Listing procedures</li><li>Maintaining minimum number of listings</li><li>Multiple listing service, relocation service or other services</li><li>Multiple offers</li><li>Putting up and taking off signs</li><li>Sales meetings and attendance</li><li>Sales teams</li><li>Screening of prospects</li><li>Servicing listings</li><li>Submitting ads</li><li>Submitting offers</li><li>Who and when associate obligates principal broker</li></ul>	<ul><li>Signing of certain documents</li><li>Splitting commissions</li><li>Storage and contents of transactions records</li><li>What manager can authorize to be spent</li><li>What associates may spend out of office funds</li><li>When company will or won't pay legal expenses</li><li>Withholding and Social Security taxes</li></ul> **Staffing/Human Resources** <ul><li>Grooming and dress</li><li>Drinking and drugs</li><li>Loyalty to firm</li><li>Insurance - health & automobile</li><li>Minimum recommended earnings</li><li>Recruiting new licensees</li><li>Requirements of persons hired</li><li>Settlement of disputes</li><li>Sexual harassment</li><li>Termination of licensees</li></ul>

If controls are properly built into the manual, managers will be able to:
- detect and correct problems while they are still manageable.
- verify that procedures are being followed, so they need only concern themselves with exceptions to the policy.

An effective manual will provide enough guidance that the associates need to ask for assistance only when the situation calls for an exception to standard policies or procedures.

A manual provides that the "company will charge 6% for residential, 8% for vacant land, 9% for commercial property, and 5% for builders. For exceptions, see the principal broker." If an associate finds a builder with 40 homes, who does not want to pay 5%, he will have to go to the manager (principal broker) to see if the company may be willing to charge only 4%. If an exception appears frequently enough, the principal broker may want to amend the manual. If the principal broker discovers most builders are refusing to pay 5% and will only pay 4%, he may amend the manual to perhaps state the commission charge for builders of more than 10 homes would be 4%.

Revisions

The manual cannot remain inflexible and rigid to the point that it is outdated and falls into disuse. If it is updated and changed as laws and rules evolve or the situation of the company changes, it will allow for incorporation of new concepts and methods. For example, in the past there was little concern about smoking in offices, sexual harassment, provisions for the disabled, and confidentiality. Today's policies and procedures manuals must deal with these issues.

For the policy manual to be workable, it will have to be revised from time to time. A principal broker will have a revision policy to provide for tracking the frequency of  exceptions, as well as the need to adapt new policies to comply with law changes. Many companies will have their policies and procedures manual reviewed periodically, perhaps once every year or every six months, either by the principal broker or by designated managers. At these times they may incorporate procedures based on new information from their Realtor® organizations, decisions resulting from disputes between associates in the company or between companies, or corrective actions that have had to be taken. Policies he does not intend to continue to follow or enforce impartially among all members of firm should be removed.

Many ideas for changes will come from sales meetings. At these meetings, associates can provide input as to:

- policies that may need to be revised.
- activities for which policies or procedures should be added to the manual.

However, the opportunity to provide input on a policy should not be seen as the ability to create the policy. Thoughts or topics that come up at the meetings should be noted and put in a file. When the principal broker has the opportunity to develop the policy, he can then present it to the associates at another meeting. At that time it can be explained, discussed, and defended against objections that might be raised, and all associates present might understand why the revised policy will benefit them.

In most cases, associates, like other human beings, initially will resist change. This means that for change to be least jarring, some advance notice of revisions must be given associates. The best timing of the notice will depend on the significance of the revision. In some cases, there is a procedure that must be changed immediately due to a law or rule change. In other instances, there may be minor changes that can be made with little advance notice or discussion. Before making major revisions, such as in agency policy or policy affecting personal transactions, there may need to be some discussion and explanation of the reasons for the change and implementation of the policy well in advance of the effective date of the change. The principal broker will usually send the proposed change to each office manager or staff manager for their comments and perhaps have meetings to discuss the change before introducing it to the associates.

Uses

The manual is valuable only if it is used.

In some companies, each associate is given a loose-leaf copy of the manual. To make sure the associate has read it, understands it, and uses it, the principal broker may require

the associate to sign an acknowledgment once a year to show that they have reviewed it. When changes are made, associates are often required to turn the manual in, so it can be amended and reissued. The associates may be required to initial each revised page, confirming that they have read it and understand it.

In other companies, the principal broker does not issue the manual to the associates but keeps a master copy in the office for reference. This avoids the problem of associates losing their copy or having an outdated manual. A more modern practice is to have the manual posted on the company's intranet website, so all associates can have access to the latest version and make copies of revised pages as needed.

The manual may have a number of valuable uses:
- It establishes company policy so all associates can provide consistent representation of the company and its objectives.
- It answers basic questions, relieving managers of the burden of restating and explaining the most common types of procedures. It does not attempt to answer questions involving difficult or unique situations. When used effectively, it provides for day-to-day handling of routine administrative procedures without the intervention of the manager.
- It creates an established authority that allows the principal broker and the managers to be more consistent.
- It helps establish and maintain good relations between associates and between associates and management, so disputes between the parties can be prevented or easily resolved.
- Where disputes cannot be prevented, the manual provides grievance procedures to clearly define how the grievance will be handled and how the decision will be made to address the grievance.
- It makes it easier to recruit new licensees and licensees from other companies. Prospective agents may be encouraged to work for a company that has its mission, purpose and objectives in writing. They will also be able to see how the company professes to deal with certain issues. For new agents, this can be reassuring. For

agents seeking to switch firms, this enables them to compare philosophy and methods of operation with their current or former firm.

- It makes it easier to train new licensees and reinforce policy and procedures for existing licensees. Policies and procedures that are in writing are easier to understand and remember and are available for associates as well as trainers to refer to for guidance.
- It is a useful tool for sales meetings. It helps clarify procedures and policies, and it encourages feedback on procedures that may need to be revised or developed.
- It is a point of reference for analyzing needed changes in procedures.
- It enables the principal broker to clearly state expectations for associates and provide specific methods of performing certain tasks.
- It helps to satisfy the legal requirement that the principal broker have written agreements and office policies, including those relating to agency relationships, implemented by the principal real estate broker with reasonable actions set forth to carry out the agreements and policies in order to show adequate supervision.

If not handled properly, a manual can cause some problems:

- If it lacks flexibility and its procedures and policies are so rigid that they cannot be changed, associates will fear acting creatively and, as a result, lose listings or sales. Procedures must be flexible to allow for the implementation of new concepts and methods.
- If it has too much flexibility, it may fail to effectively serve as a guide.
- If it is not periodically reviewed, the policies and procedures are likely to become obsolete and provide no or incorrect guidance.

----- SAMPLE MANUAL -----

ABC BROKERAGE POLICIES AND PROCEDURES

PURPOSE OF THIS MANUAL

The purpose of this manual is to set forth basic policies and general guidelines to be followed in the day-to-day operation of ABC Realty. It will not cover every incident or answer every question. In any matter not covered by this manual, the principal broker will decide and be guided in such decisions by company policy, experience, the Realtors® Code of Ethics, the Bylaws of the Oregon Association of Realtors® and local Association of Realtors®, the Multiple Listing Service Rules, and the laws and regulations of the Real Estate Agency. From time to time additions and revisions will be made to this manual, effective after reasonable notice. A copy of this manual is always available for reference in the office.

One important goal of ABC Realty is to provide the greatest possible opportunity for personal and economic satisfaction for its associates. However, the success of each associate is dependent on his efforts.

OBJECTIVE OF ABC REALTY

The objective of ABC Realty is to make a profit through integrity, high principles, and a commitment to obtain positive results for ABC Realty clients. Associates are expected to uphold the reputation of ABC Realty.

ACTIVITY LOG

An activity log is maintained at the receptionist's desk in order to provide the manager and associates with information useful in analyzing the effectiveness of advertising efforts. Floor duty associates are to record all incoming floor calls in the log and sign the log at the end of their floor duty shift.

AGREEMENTS

- Always have parties read all agreements affecting their rights and obligations. Ask if they understood all provisions, and explain those that can be explained in nonlegal terms. Recommend legal advice where questions relate to legal matters or interpretation.
- Immediately give a copy of any document the person is signing to that person.
- Submit all documents to the manager for review within seven banking days of their acceptance.

ATTORNEYS

Associates are to refrain from offering legal advice and should strongly recommend that all parties involved in a transaction obtain the services of an independent attorney.

ATTORNEY FEES

If ABC Realty engages outside counsel in any dispute or litigation resulting from a transaction in which an associate is involved:

- All legal fees and court costs and deposition expense shall be shared by the associate and the principal broker on the basis of their percentage of the commission in the transaction. The associate's share of these costs is due and payable as costs are incurred.
- If an associate hires his own counsel for representation in a dispute or litigation, he shall not be obligated for any further outside counsel fees and legal expenses, upon written notification to the principal broker. However, the associate will not be relieved from his obligation to share a proportionate amount of the costs of compromise settlements or judgments against the principal broker.
- The manager will handle all calls to an attorney retained by the principal broker. An associate may not call the attorney directly.

AUTHORITY OF ASSOCIATES

Associates have no authority to bind or commit ABC to any contract, promise or course of action without the prior written authorization of the principal broker. Associates are authorized to execute listing contracts and other approved documents on behalf of the principal broker, but they have no authority to vary commission terms from those previously approved by the principal broker without prior approval of the principal broker.

AUTOMOBILE

Associates shall furnish and pay all expenses for their own automobile. The principal broker is to be furnished with a memorandum showing the name of the insurer, policy dates, type of coverage, and limits of liability for bodily injury and property damage of at least $100,000/$300,000. (However, $250,000/$1,000,000 coverage is recommended.) ABC Realty is to be named as an "Additional Named Insured" in all policies.

BOARD OF REALTORS®

Every associate must join the appropriate Board of Realtors® immediately at their own expense.

BUSINESS CALLS

ABC Realty furnishes telephone service in the office to all associates. Phone conversations should be limited to a few minutes, so calls should not be placed on hold while actions need to be taken or decisions need to be made.

BUSINESS CARDS

All business cards will be paid for by the associate, but must be approved by the principal broker and conform to the requirements of the principal broker.

CLOSING PROCEDURES

The last person out of the office will be responsible for:

- Turning off the coffee machine, the photocopier, and all lights except night-lights.
- Locking all doors and, when appropriate, verifying that both outside doors are locked.

COMMISSION DISPUTES

The principal broker reserves the right to determine commission splits in the event of a dispute between two associates. Most disputes can be avoided by making prearrangements in writing.

COMMISSION SCHEDULE (for associates not on a desk fee arrangement)

In-house Transaction

    Annual

Level	Earnings	ABC Share	Listing/Selling Agent
1	0 - $ 9,999	45%	27.5%
2	10 - 19,000	42.5%	28.75%
3	20 - 29,999	40%	30%
4	30 - 39,999	35%	32.5%
5	Over 40,000	30%	35%

ABC listing/Cooperating broker sale (55/45)

Level	Earnings	ABC Share	Listing/Selling Agent
1	0 - $ 9,999	27.5%	27.5%
2	10 - 19,999	27%	28%
3	20 - 29,999	26.5%	28.5%
4	30 - 39,999	26%	29%
5	Over 40,000	25%	30%

Cooperating broker listing/ABC sale (55/45)

Level	Earnings	ABC Share	Listing/Selling Agent
1	0 - $ 9,999	22.5%	22.5%
2	10 - 19,999	22.5%	22.5%
3	over 20,000	20%	25%

All commission splits are calculated based on gross commission dollars paid to the associate at the time the transaction is written. Associates begin each year one level below the level of closed commissions earned the previous year. Upon termination for any reason, the commission schedule in Level 1 will apply on all closings after the date of termination less any shared costs associated with closing the transaction as determined by the principal broker.

COMPLAINTS AGAINST OTHER BROKER OFFICES
Complaints against other offices should be discussed with the principal broker, not with buyers, sellers, or other associates.

CONDUCT
All associates are independent business people and entitled to respect. Associates should be cooperative and helpful with each other. Conduct in the offices and in the performance of duties on behalf of ABC should be professional.

CONFERENCE ROOMS
Conference rooms are to be used when meeting with clients and customers, presenting or reviewing offers, meeting with other associates from other companies, making confidential phone calls or when silence is mandatory. The manager's office is available when both conference rooms are being used.

CONFIDENTIAL INFORMATION
A client file, marked "Confidential," will be opened for each client as soon as an agency relationship is established. All active client and transaction files must be maintained by the manager. Access to active files will be limited to assure confidentiality. All confidential client information will be kept in client files, which will be kept separate from transaction files. Transaction files may not contain confidential client information. Associates may not discuss confidential information with anyone who does not have an agency relationship with the client, including other associates.

COOPERATION WITH OTHER COMPANIES
ABC Realty policy is to cooperate with other real estate professionals to the extent allowed by the seller. Unless the seller instructs otherwise, each listing is to be made available to other brokers,

including buyer brokers, on a cooperative basis, under terms consistent with the seller's instructions. Associates shall bring to their principal broker's immediate attention any offer or request by another broker or agent to "co-list" a property. Associates may not enter into, or encourage, "co-listing" arrangements without the express authorization of their principal broker.

DESIGNATED AGENCY

In a transaction where the buyer for property listed by an associate is represented by another associate supervised by the listing associate's principal broker, the principal broker will represent both the seller and the buyer, pursuant to a Disclosed Limited Agency Agreement. The listing and buyer's associates will continue to represent only their respective parties, as agreed to by each party in a Disclosed Limited Agency Agreement. All representation must be in accord with company policies and procedures, preventing access to confidential information concerning another client involved in the same transaction. Failure to follow these policies and procedures is grounds for termination of the associate's Independent Contractor Agreement.

DISCLOSED LIMITED AGENCY

An associate may act in a transaction as an agent of both the buyer and the seller, or as an agent of two buyers competing for the same property, only after fully explaining disclosed limited agency relationships, including the role of the principal broker, and obtaining Disclosed Limited Agency Agreements from both parties. All signed Disclosed Limited Agency Agreements must be attached as an addendum to any written agency agreement between the buyer and the associate. Associates must honor all duties imposed on disclosed limited agents, including the preservation of the lawful confidences of each party.

DISCRIMINATION

No ABC associate shall discriminate against any person based on race, creed, color, religion, national origin, sex, marital status, familial status, handicap, source of income (unless illegal income), or sexual orientation.

DRESS CODE

Associates are encouraged to dress in a businesslike fashion. Visits to the office on a day off in leisure attire should be short to avoid giving an impression of a lack of professionalism in the office.

EQUIPMENT/SUPPLIES

ABC Realty will provide associates with the necessary equipment to do their job. This equipment should not be used for personal use. Office equipment, supplies, reference materials, etc, shall not be removed from the office without permission of the manager. Materials deemed necessary to complete a real estate transaction outside the office are excluded.

Upon termination of an associate's association with ABC Realty, all equipment, supplies, keys and reference materials must be returned to the office.

Company computer equipment, including laptops, may not be used for personal use, including word processing and computing functions. Associates shall not install any other programs to a company computer without the written permission of the manager or principal broker. Forbidden programs include games, online services, screen savers, etc. Associates shall not copy programs installed on company computers unless specifically directed to do so in writing by the manager. The telephone lines at ABC Realty must remain open for business calls and to service clients and customers. Associates are requested to discourage personal calls, incoming and outgoing, with the exception of emergency calls.

ETHICS

In the real estate business, ethics, moral principles, and quality of practice govern the professional relationship with prospective buyers and sellers and with fellow agents. ABC's ethics represent its honesty, integrity, and spirit of proper conduct.

ABC Realty is a member of the National Association of REALTORS®, the state Association of REALTORS®, the local Board of REALTORS®, and the Multiple Listing Service. Associates must make application for membership in the above organizations.

EXPENSES

In general, associates are responsible for the following expenses:

1. Automobile
2. Club or organizational fees or dues
3. Insurance
4. Multiple listing dues
5. Individual map books
6. Glue sticks
7. Binders
8. Pens and pencils/tablets
9. Any card file system
10. Keys
11. Personalized sign riders
12. General office supplies
13. Realtor dues, license fees, accreditation fees
14. Express or overnight mailing

ABC will furnish:

1. Stationery and envelopes for correspondence
2. Preprinted broker promotional material
3. Copy machine printing

FARM PROGRAMS

A farm program consists of a specific geographic area of about 300 homes in which an associate can concentrate continual efforts. Associates will be assigned exclusive farm areas in which they can focus efforts. A quarterly mailing is required for an associate to retain a farm area.

Other associates may make sales and list properties, though, based on For Sale By Owners, expired listings, withdrawals, referrals, and past clients in farm areas of other associates.

FLYERS

As a general rule, associates will pay any expense associated with the printing of special flyers. The manager's approval is required for all printed flyers prior to actual printing. All flyers prepared for ABC Realty listing must:

- Comply with nondiscrimination policy
- Display the federal fair housing logo
- Display the company name, phone number and logo
- Display the associate's name
- Conform to the manager's guidelines and policies

FLOOR DUTY ASSIGNMENT

Floor duty is voluntary. To be assigned floor duty, the associate must request it in writing. To remain on floor duty, the associate must be on time and complete a full shift; use their best efforts to obtain results from each call; make sure their assigned time is covered in the event they cannot fulfill their scheduled shift.

A customer who asks for a particular associate by name shall be referred to that associate if the associate is in the office or immediately available. All others shall be directed to the floor associate. If it is later determined that the customer was procured by an associate whose name was not mentioned or forgotten (farm mailer, etc.) the associates involved shall discuss and negotiate the commission with the manager.

The floor schedule will be prepared one week prior to the end of each month. The manager must be informed of vacations or absences prior to the schedule being published. After the schedule is distributed it will be the associate's responsibility to make trades or changes. Sickness or emergencies will be the only excuse for nonattendance of floor time.

HOLIDAYS

ABC Realty observes the following holidays each year:
New Year's Day
Memorial Day
Independence Day
Labor Day
Thanksgiving Day
Friday after Thanksgiving Day
Christmas Day

KEYS

Always ask the owner to furnish two keys: one for emergencies and one for the lockbox. Prior to closing, keys to all lockable doors, including garage, padlock, and gates are to be available. Keys are not to be given to purchasers, pending the closing of a sale without the written permission from the seller. Keys may be given to appraisers as authorized by the seller.

When using a key an associate must, before leaving any property they have shown, check all doors and windows to determine that they are securely locked or fastened.

LEAD-BASED PAINT DISCLOSURE

The listing agent will determine at the time of listing whether property being sold as a residence was constructed before 1978. If it was, he will have the seller complete and sign a Lead-Based Paint Disclosure Addendum, provide the disclosure to each buyer for their signature at the earliest possible time, and make it part of the sale agreement for the property.

LEGAL ADVICE

Associates must not give legal advice, directly or indirectly. This includes advice regarding the legal rights of the parties, the legal effect of notices and instruments and matters affecting the title. The response to any question that might border on legal advice must be that only attorneys may give such advice and/or information.

LISTINGS

ABC Realty requires that listings be exclusive right to sell, for a minimum 120-day period at six percent (6%) percent commission. New home sales, builder and developer activity, and condominium developments are normally at five percent (5%) commission. Commissions and time periods can be negotiated for higher-priced properties, with manager approval. Net listings, joint listings, and co-listings with other brokers cannot be taken.

During the term of a listing, the listing agent will have contact at least weekly with the seller to keep the seller informed. Associates shall arrange timely presentation of offers, attempt to meet the selling agent, before the principals are confronted, to clarify any points and allow the selling agent to present the offer with a minimum of interruption. The listing agent shall prepare a net-sheet for the client.

The seller will make the decision to accept, reject, or make a counteroffer. The listing agent can only guide him. If the seller wishes to reject an offer, the listing agent should attempt to convince the seller that a counteroffer should be prepared, since some buyers will accept a realistic counteroffer even if they have made an unacceptable initial offer.

Upon acceptance, the listing agent will assure all parties receive copies of documents, initialed and signed where needed.

Throughout the transaction, associates shall monitor compliance with all contingencies, check the preliminary title report for irregularities and discrepancies and discuss them with the manager and the title officer, and maintain close relationships with all involved. Associates shall attend the closing.

LONG-DISTANCE PHONE CALLS
ABC will pay for long-distance calls for business purposes. Each month associates will review a copy of their long-distance bill, report any discrepancies, and reimburse the principal broker for any personal calls.

MAIL PROCEDURES
ABC will pay for the normal cost of business mail, but not for overnight express. Associates shall not mail personal letters through the office unless the exact postage is prepaid. Overnight service should be reimbursed by the client at the close of the transaction.

MULTIPLE CONCURRENT OFFERS
When more than one offer is physically received on a listing prior to the first offer being accepted and: (1) one or more of the offers originates through the listing associate, the manager will be present representing the seller when each offer is submitted, or (2) none of the offers originates through the listing associate, the listing associate shall be present to represent the seller. Exceptions to this rule must be approved by the manager.

Prior to submitting any multiple offers, the associate shall notify the seller that more than one offer will be presented and they should defer any decision until all offers have been presented. At the presentation of each offer, only the seller, listing associate (or manager), and the associate with the offer should be present.

After all offers have been presented, the seller should be advised that they may accept one of the offers "as is" (make no changes), counter the offer they consider the best, or propose other instructions. They should be advised to take no action on the other offers until they complete negotiation on the chosen offer.

If the seller insists on making simultaneous multiple counteroffers, the manager should be notified, and the following language must be used: "This counteroffer is being made with the understanding that it is being made to more than one prospective buyer and that acceptance hereof shall be of no force or effect until the acceptance of buyer is both delivered in writing to the seller and is acknowledged by the seller in writing."

MULTIPLE LISTING SERVICE

MLS membership is mandatory and associates must attend the orientation classes for instruction in the use of the computer terminal and forms. Monthly dues are due the 1st of each month.

NONSOLICITATION OF OTHER BROKERS' LISTINGS

At no time during an exclusive listing of another broker shall an associate discuss with the owner anything regarding the benefits of listing with ABC. In the event a seller asks ABC Realty or its associate to talk with them regarding a listing prior to the expiration of another broker's listing, associates must, regardless of the circumstances, follow the REALTOR® Code of Ethics and rules of the MLS. Avoid casual remarks to owners about the service provided by other brokers. These remarks have a way of getting back to listing brokers, often out of context.

OFFICE APPEARANCE

This is a smoke-free office. Associates are responsible for keeping it neat and orderly.

OFFICE HOURS

During daylight savings time, office hours will be 8:30 a.m. to 7:00 p.m., Monday through Friday; 9:00 a.m. to 6:00 p.m., Saturday and Sunday.

During standard time, office hours are 8:30 a.m. to 6:00 p.m., Monday through Friday; 9:00 a.m. to 5:00 p.m. on Saturday and Sunday.

PERSONAL ASSISTANTS

Associates may hire personal assistants to assist them in their business activities only upon an express written agreement with the principal broker. Those assistants who will engage in professional real estate activity must be licensed in this state.

Associates may employ, or otherwise engage, unlicensed personal assistants, who would be the sole responsibility of the hiring associate. The hiring associate must supervise the unlicensed assistant's activities and satisfy all employer duties with regard to the assistant. An unlicensed assistant may not be paid any portion of a real estate commission. While not the assistant's employer, the principal broker may supervise an unlicensed assistant's activities in order to prevent the assistant from engaging in unlicensed professional real estate activity.

Associates with licensed assistants must obtain a principal broker's license, enter a written Broker Associate/Licensed Personal Assistant Agreement with the licensed assistant, supervise the licensed assistant under a Divided Control and Supervision Agreement with the principal broker, and enter into a separate Principal broker/Broker Associate Licensed Personal Assistant Agreement with the principal broker. An associate who engages a licensed personal assistant may pay the assistant directly, consistent with the engaging associate's Independent Contractor Agreement, office policy and state law. Associates are responsible for ensuring professional fees or necessary dues are paid.

A licensed personal assistant may not establish any agency relationship with a client that is different than the agency relationship between the hiring associate and the client.

PRINCIPAL BROKER - ASSOCIATE RELATIONSHIP
Each associate is required to follow all requirements of ORS 696 and OAR 863.

RELATIONS WITH OTHER ASSOCIATES
Associates are to conduct themselves in a professional, courteous, and cooperative manner in their relations with other associates and use their best efforts to promote their own and the principal broker's businesses.

Associates should resolve personal disagreements not involving real estate transactions, office procedures or policies, or real estate rules and laws between themselves without disrupting office operations, interfering with the transaction of professional real estate activity, or involving other associates or the principal broker. However, the principal broker is available to informally assist in resolving these disagreements.

The associate's principal broker will decide any dispute among or between associates with respect to this manual's policies and procedures or the Independent Contractor Agreement. Any dispute involving a real estate transaction or application of real estate laws or rules is to be immediately brought to the attention of the associate's principal broker and resolved in accordance with applicable real estate rules and law. Decisions by the principal broker are final but are not intended to alter any policies, contractual provisions, or laws.

SALE OR PURCHASE OF ASSOCIATE'S PROPERTY
When buying or selling property through ABC Realty, full-time associates may act as brokers in the transaction, provided they fully disclose their license status in writing in the sales agreement and escrow instructions in the following manner: "The parties hereto agree that the seller/buyer is an associate of ABC Realty, is representing himself as the seller/buyer in the transaction, and will receive a portion of any real estate commission paid to ABC Realty in this transaction."

For the sale of their primary residence through ABC Realty, associates who have been with ABC Realty for at least one year and are not on a desk-fee arrangement will receive a reduction of 70% of the commission received by the principal broker after deducting commissions paid to associates and cooperating brokers. If an associate has not been with ABC Realty one year, the amount to which they would be entitled will be released from escrow at their one year anniversary date if they are licensed with ABC Realty at that time. When the buyer and seller of a primary residence are both associates, the principal broker's share of the commission will be waived and shared equally between the buyer and seller.

All transactions involving a commission rebate will be presented through the manager or an associate designated by him.

SELLER'S PROPERTY DISCLOSURE
The listing agent must explain the seller's duties with respect to the property disclosure form and have the seller agree to deliver the form to each buyer who makes a written offer. When the disclosure form is filled out by the seller, the listing agent will review the form and bring to the client's attention any discrepancies reasonably apparent to the associate after a noninvasive walk-through inspection of the property.

SEXUAL HARASSMENT
No employees or associates may engage in any conduct constituting sexual harassment, or seek reprisal against any person charging them with such conduct. "Sexual harassment" includes any

unwelcome sexual advance, request for sexual favors or other verbal or physical conduct of a sexual nature or with sexual overtones, such as offensive comments and jokes, profanity, lewd gestures, unwanted physical contact, and exhibit of sexually explicit or suggestive materials. Any employee or associate who observes an act of sexual harassment must report the act to the manager or principal broker, who will conduct a full and fair investigation, and take all necessary steps to remedy the situation and prevent any reoccurrence of any harassment.

SHOWING PROPERTY – OTHER OFFICES

Associates shall treat the listing broker's sellers as if they were their own. When showing a property, they shall not discuss the listing price or other broker with the owner. They shall not contact owners regarding offers, and shall submit all offers through the listing broker and not directly to the seller. The ethics of another broker are not to be discussed with anyone other than the principal broker.

SIGNS

It is the listing agent's responsibility to erect his own signs. At the expiration of the listing or after the property has sold (allowing a reasonable length of time for the sold rider exposure), the sign should be returned to the office. Name riders are the associate's expense and must conform to the principal broker's requirements and policy.

TERMINATION POLICY

The manager will determine whether or not an associate is exerting an effort commensurate with the associate's ability. At least once a year each associate will have a formal performance appraisal with the manager to rate progress and performance. An associate may also discuss progress any time they feel the need.

Termination procedures will be governed by the principal broker-associate contract, but commissions and referral fees due the associate will be largely determined on a case-by-case basis by the manager.

TOUR OF NEW LISTINGS

Tours will be conducted in a group immediately following the weekly sales meetings. The listing associate has the duty to schedule a tour. This means he must complete the tour request information and give it to the receptionist, set up an appointment, provide access to the property, conduct the tour and answer questions, introduce the other associates to any owners present, provide tour feedback to the owner the same day, and thank the owner.

WORK HABITS

ABC associates are part of a team, contributing their share to the business in the office by:
- being present and on time at all office meetings, weekly or educational, principal broker-sponsored seminars.
- being punctual for all floor time or notifying the manager of a replacement.
- soliciting listings to maintain a quality and properly priced inventory for the benefit of principal broker.
- establishing and maintaining transaction records.
- endeavoring to serve all clients and customers, and cooperate with fellow associates and other brokers in a professional manner so as to enhance the reputation of the office and principal broker.

----- COMPANY POLICY FOR PRIVATE TRANSACTIONS -----

The law does not require an active licensee to have his principal broker list his property for sale or represent him as a buyer's representative in purchase transactions.

However, regardless of whether a principal broker acts as an agent for a licensee in personal transactions, the principal broker remains responsible under the license law for supervising such personal transactions. This means that the principal broker should be informed of the licensee's intent to engage in a personal transaction. He must review all transaction documents to ensure that the associate adheres to the same duty to deal honestly and in good faith with an unrepresented party that he has in a transaction in which he represents a client.

Most principal brokers have written company policies relating to personal transactions and include provisions relating to any compensation resulting from these transactions in their independent contractor agreements.

Financial Reports

In order to ensure he can meet financial obligations as they become due, a principal broker must not only have sufficient capital to meet his needs, but must use that capital wisely. Financial reports enable the principal broker to determine whether he has been using that capital wisely.

----- BALANCE SHEETS -----

A **balance sheet** shows the financial condition of the business on a given date, often at the close of business at the end of a fiscal year, or at the end of a month or a quarter. It sets forth the amounts of the company's assets, liabilities, and capital (also called net worth or owner's equity) in two columns. Assets are listed on one side and the liabilities and net worth on the other. The total of the assets will equal, or balance with, the total of the liabilities and net worth, creating what is called the basic accounting equation.

Basic Accounting Equation

Assets = Liabilities + Net Worth
($1,000,000) = ($700,000) + ($300,000)

Assets – Liabilities = Net Worth
($1,000,000) - ($700,000) = ($300,000)

Assets – Net Worth = Liabilities
($1,000,000) - ($300,000) = ($700,000)

Assets

An **asset** is anything of value owned by the business, whether it is owned free and clear or subject to a loan.

> **For Example**
>
> A building with a mortgage against it or equipment being purchased on an installment plan would be considered assets. Therefore, a $100,000 building owned free and clear is a $100,000 asset, and a $100,000 building with a mortgage balance of $80,000 against it is still a $100,000 asset.

Assets can be tangible (physical) or intangible (e.g., rights). They can include such items as prepaid rent, prepaid insurance, land, buildings, equipment, notes and accounts receivable, furniture, fixtures, and the value of a franchise or a franchise name.

Balance Sheet

ASSETS		LIABILITIES	
Cash		Accounts Payable	____
Accounts Receivable	____	Notes Payable	____
Inventory	____	Wages/Commissions Payable	____
Prepaid Expenses	____	Taxes Payable	____
Total Current Assets	____	Current Portion Long-Term Debt	____
		Total Current Liabilities	____
Land	____	Mortgages Payable	____
Building & Equipment	____	Contracts Payable	____
Less Depreciation	(____)	Bonds Payable	____
Intangibles	____	Owner Loans	____
Other Assets	____	**Total Fixed Liabilities**	____
Total Fixed Assets	____		

OWNER'S EQUITY (NET WORTH)

		Owner's Investment (Capital Stock)	____
		Capital Contributions	____
		Net Profit	____
		Less Withdrawals	____
		Retained Earnings	____
		Total Net Worth	____
Total Assets	____	**Total Liabilities and Net Worth**	____

Assets may be shown on a balance sheet as either current assets or fixed assets. **Current assets** are cash and those assets which in the normal course of business will be converted into cash within one year from the date of the balance sheet. These are usually listed in the order of liquidity, that is, their ability to be transformed to cash.

Under current assets, the balance sheet would show cash, followed by accounts and notes receivable that are expected to be collected in the near future. Current assets would also include a company's inventory of supplies and prepaid expenses, such as the unconsumed portion of prepaid insurance, rent, interest, property taxes, and long-term advertising.

> **For Example**
>
> If rent and insurance had been paid through June of the following year, a balance sheet prepared as of the prior December 31 would show six months of rent and insurance as current assets of the company.

Fixed assets are assets that are expected to be useful to the business over several years. They were not purchased for resale purposes and will usually not be sold, as long as their economic usefulness continues. These would include land, buildings, equipment, furniture, fixtures and goodwill. Fixed assets are usually shown on the balance sheet at cost.

The total assets are the sum of the current assets and the fixed assets.

Total Assets = Current Assets + Fixed Assets

Liabilities

On the other side of the balance sheet are liabilities and net worth. Liabilities (or debts) are claims of others to the total assets of the business. They are obligations of the company to pay money or other assets, or to render services, to others, such as taxing authorities, trade suppliers, employees, and financial institutions.

Current liabilities will mature within one year from the date of the balance sheet, such as accounts payable, notes payable, wages and/or commissions payable, taxes payable, and the amount due within a year on long-term debts. **Fixed liabilities** mature over a longer period of time than one year (such as mortgages payable, long-term contracts, and bonds payable).

Net Worth (Owner's Equity)

Net worth (or the owner's equity) is the difference between the total assets and the total liabilities. Under net worth, the balance sheet may show, as of the beginning of the year, the owner's investment, or the capital stock if it is a corporation, and any additional capital contributions made by the owner to the business during the year. It will also show the company's net profit and withdrawals. Withdrawals are money taken out  of the business by the owner for personal use or to pay taxes, or for a corporation, money paid to stockholders in the form of dividends. The amount remaining after deducting the withdrawals from the profit is called retained earnings. The net worth of the company is the sum of the capital invested in the company plus retained earnings.

Net Worth =
Total Assets – Total Liabilities
Capital Invested + Retained Earnings

Solvency

Solvency is the company's ability to pay bills. To be solvent, a company must have working capital to pay its bills. **Working capital** is the money left over after paying current liabilities from current assets.

Working Capital = Current Assets - Current Liabilities

When working capital is too low, it may be necessary for the principal broker to invest additional capital or borrow more on a long-term basis. Often the cause for working capital deficiency is unprofitable performance. The reasons for such nonprofitability can generally be found in an analysis of the income and expense statement.

On the other hand, too much working capital may not be good either. Current assets are largely unproductive. Cash in a checking account earns little or no interest. Accounts receivable indicate other people are using the principal broker's money with no return to him, or with a return that is less than what he might be able to earn on his own investments. If working capital is excessive, consideration should be given to investing excess cash or to paying off long-term debts to save interest expense.

Ratios to Test Solvency

Two financial ratios are often used to test the solvency of a company:
1. Current ratio
2. Quick (or acid-test) ratio

The **current ratio** measures the ability of the company to pay its current debts with cash or near cash. It is determined by dividing the company's current assets by its current liabilities.

Current Ratio = Current Assets ÷ Current Liabilities

The higher the ratio, the more liquid the company's position is and, therefore, the greater the company's ability to borrow money.

The **quick ratio** (or acid-test) ratio reflects the company's ability to meet its current obligations with quickly convertible assets should its revenues suddenly cease or drop. This ratio is determined by dividing the company's quick assets by its current liabilities. **Quick assets** are assets that can quickly be converted to cash, such as cash and accounts receivable.

Quick (Acid-Test) Ratio =
Quick Assets (Cash + Accounts Receivable) ÷ Current Liabilities

Safety

Each company has a different level of risk. In the measurement of a company's degree of safety, debt-to-equity and debt coverage ratios are used to help determine the company's ability to at least repay its debt.

The **debt-to-equity ratio** is determined by dividing the total debt by the company's equity, or net worth. Generally, the higher this ratio, the riskier the business is, and the lower its credit rating will be.

$$\text{Debt-To-Equity Ratio} = \text{Total Debt} \div \text{Equity}$$

The **debt coverage ratio** uses data from the income and expense statement as well as the balance sheet. It is calculated by dividing the company's total net profit plus noncash expenses by its outstanding debt. This ratio shows the ability of the company to repay its debt out of cash profits, as well as to take on additional debt.

$$\text{Debt Coverage Ratio} =$$
$$(\text{Net Profit} + \text{Noncash Expenses}) \div \text{Outstanding Debt}$$

----- INCOME STATEMENTS -----

The **income statement** (also called a profit and loss statement, an income and expense statement, or an operating statement) shows the company's income and expenses, or profit or loss for a given period; often a month, a quarter, or a year. The difference between the company's gross income and its expenses is its net profit or loss for the period.

On this form, income (also called gross dollar or revenue) is the total of all payments, commissions, fees, and other income for the brokerage. It measures the firm's volume of business, but it does not reflect the firm's profitability. Profitability is the amount of the gross income not paid out in expenses.

From the gross revenue received, the principal broker will split the commissions with his associates and cooperating brokers, and pay fees to franchisors, relocation services, and multiple listing services.

Income Statement

Income (commissions and fees)		$ ____
Distribution Costs (commission splits)	____	
Gross Income (company dollar)		$ ____
Operating Expenses	____	
Salary Expenses		____
Technology and Communications Expenses	____	
Occupancy Expenses	____	
Selling Expenses	____	
Advertising Expenses	____	
Total Operating Expenses		$ ____
Earnings before interest and taxes (EBIT)		$ ____
Interest on loan		____
Income Taxes	____	
Net Income from Continuing Operations		$ ____
Gross Income (Company Dollar)		$ ____
Total Expenses	____	
Owner's return on company dollar	$ ____	
Less value of owner's services (paid to owner)		____
Net return on company dollar		$ ____

Deduction of commission splits and service fees results in the company's gross income or company dollar. The **company dollar** is the portion of the revenue that belongs to the firm before operations costs and expenses are deducted. The company dollar indicates the amount of business done by the company but does not indicate profitability. For purposes of analysis, all other expenses and costs are compared to the company dollar.

> **For Example**
>
> A principal broker had gross income of $1,500,000. After he paid out $800,000 in commission splits and other fees, he was left with $700,000 as the company dollar. In any financial analysis, his expenses would be compared to the company dollar (the $700,000) in order to obtain an operating ratio, or expense ratio.

Operating (Expense) Ratio = Expenses ÷ Company Dollar

An analysis of expenses will consider the distribution of fixed expenses and variable expenses. **Fixed expenses** are those that remain constant. The company may pay them regardless of how much or how little business it does. They include office rent, equipment rental, yellow pages advertising, salary for a receptionist, depreciation, property taxes, insurance, association dues, and the like.

Variable expenses (e.g., commissions) are tied directly to the amount of business done, so they increase or decrease as the company's business increases or decreases.

Operating expenses include license fees, dues, insurance premiums, legal and accounting fees, taxes, repair or rental of equipment, office supplies, printing, maps, plats, and photography, interest on business loans, bad debts, postage, auto expense, and others.

Salary expense includes salaries of managers, clerical and other staff, such as bookkeepers, payroll taxes, and any employee benefits.

Technology and communications expense includes telephone service and call charges, tech support, service contracts, and other related communication services, such as company cell phones. It does not include yellow pages or directory listing charges.

Occupancy expenses pertain to rent, utilities, and janitorial service and maintenance.

Selling expense includes training, conferences and courses, travel and conventions, entertainment, contributions, and service activities, including service clubs, sales awards, contests, testimonials, promotional gifts to clients and prospects, and similar expenses.

Advertising expense applies to the cost of advertising properties listed for sale, promoting company goodwill, and institutional advertising to promote the services offered by the company.

When total expenses are subtracted from the company dollar, the remainder is the owner's return on the company dollar. When the owner deducts the cost (salaries, bonuses, and profits) or value of the services performed by him and partners, he has the net return on the investment of the company dollar.

Profitability Ratios

The dollar amounts on the income and expense statement can be converted to ratios to measure the profitability of the company. The owner's **return on the company dollar** and the net return on the company dollar would both demonstrate the percentage of the company dollar that is profit before income taxes, and can be compared to previous experience of the company as well as industry figures.

Owner's Return on Company Dollar = Owner's Return ÷ Company Dollar

Net Return on Company Dollar = Net Return ÷ Company Dollar

If the company is involved in providing more than one service, such as residential sales and property management, or has a number of branch offices, separate profitability ratio analyses should be made of each service and branch to show the relative contribution of each, the relative burden of each, and which are profitable and which are losing money.

A **sales growth ratio** shows the percentage increase (or decrease) in sales between two time periods. It is determined by subtracting last year's sales from the current year's sales, and dividing the difference by last year's sales.

Sales Growth Ratio = (Current Year's Sales – Last Year's Sales) ÷ Last Year's Sales

Other profitability ratios use information from both the balance sheet and the profit and loss statement. The ratio for **return on assets** measures how efficiently profits are being generated from the assets of the company. It is determined by dividing the net profit by the total assets of the company. The higher the ratio, the more efficiently the assets are being used to generate a profit.

Return On Assets Ratio = Net Profit ÷ Total Assets

The **return on investments** ratio is determined by dividing the net profit by the net worth. This will help the principal broker determine whether his funds are returning a percentage of profit better than that available from other investments.

Return On Investments Ratio = Net Profit ÷ Net Worth

----- BUDGETING -----

While financial statements can tell a person where he has been, in order to find out where he will be going financially, he needs a budget.

A **budget** is a detailed plan of future receipts and expenditures, a projected profit and loss statement. A budget enables the principal broker to set a goal and list the steps needed to reach that goal. Budgeting requires him to:
- consider his basic objectives, policies, plans, and resources.
- ensure his company is properly organized.
- coordinate with his management team a comprehensive and informative effort to achieve common objectives.
- ensure that there are proper companywide controls and procedures.

Although it is usually prepared for a one-year period, a budget can be prepared to cover practically any period of time. Once a budget has been completed, the principal broker can compare actual results to goals. Budgeting enables a principal broker to analyze past performance and incorporate planned changes in operations and market conditions in order to project future income and expenses, based on a break-even analysis.

In establishing and analyzing budgets there are three very helpful tools:

1. Cost per sale
2. Income per sale
3. Break-even analysis

The cost- and income-per-sale figures provide useful measures to determine the average profitability of a sale:

- **Cost per sale** is determined by dividing the total company expenses for a period of time (often a year) by the number of sales for that period. Expenses are all expenses incurred during that period, less commissions and fees paid out to associates, other brokers, etc.

Cost per Sale =
Total Company Expenses (period Z) ÷ Number of Sales (period Z)

- **Income per sale** is determined by dividing the company dollar by the number of sales for the same period the cost of sale was determined. The difference between the cost per sale and income per sale is the profit or loss per sale for that period. These figures let the principal broker see if his profit per sale is too small or if his costs per sale are too high.

Income per Sale =
Company Dollar ÷ Number of Sales (period Z)

The **profit per sale** should increase with each sale made, since a sale will only affect variable expenses, and not fixed expenses. While commission rates could be established using the cost-per-sale figure, the determination as to whether or not a sale will contribute to profit would be based on analyzing the variable costs associated with that sale.

To analyze variable expenses the principal broker may perform a **break-even analysis**, in which he would determine the level of sales necessary to cover costs, so he may better:

- make decisions regarding commission rates, expense control, and expansion.
- determine the sales volume needed to make a reasonable profit.
- determine the sales increase necessary to generate the same profit if costs increase.
- determine the volume of sales necessary to increase his profit by a desired percentage.
- determine how much of a sales decrease would result in a loss.
- determine the impact of changes in commission structures.

One method of break-even analysis is to:

- separate fixed expenses and variable expenses based on actual experience and provide projections for future expenses.
- determine a variable cost percentage by dividing the variable expense total by the revenue.

- determine the contribution margin percentage. This is the difference between the revenue and the variable costs expressed as a percentage of the revenue. If the variable cost ratio were 40%, the contribution margin percentage would be 100% - 40%, or 60%.
- calculate the break-even sales volume by dividing the contribution margin into the fixed expense total. If there is $250,000 in fixed expenses and the contribution margin percentage is 60%, the break-even sales volume would be $250,000 ÷ 60% = $416,667.

----- TAXES AND PAYROLL RECORDS -----

The principal broker or property manager must promptly pay federal and state taxes and charges for the business, and keep complete and accurate records of all business dealings to support any deductions and expenses claimed on tax returns.

Federal Taxes

A business with employees or a Keogh Plan, or one which pays excise taxes on a tax form to the IRS, needs to file Form SS-4 with the IRS to get an employer identification number (EIN). On the federal level, the principal broker must:
- withhold from employees' wages, federal withholding tax and their portion of Medicare and Social Security premiums.
- pay federal unemployment tax (FUTA).
- pay an amount matching the employee's share for Social Security tax and Medicare tax.

For federal withholding tax, an employer must have each employee file an Employee's Withholding Allowance Certificate (IRS Form W-4). This shows his marital status and number of dependents, which is needed to determine the amount of federal income tax to withhold.

By January 31 following the end of the tax year, an employer must furnish two copies of the withholding statement (Form W-2) to each employee from whom taxes have been withheld and send a Form 1099 to any business that provided services where compensation was not subject to withholding (such as an independent contractor).

Form W-3, summarizing the W-2s, and Form 1096, summarizing the 1099s, must be sent to the IRS by the last day in February for the preceding year.

Employers must file Form 941, Employer's Quarterly Federal Tax Return, for federal income withholding tax, Social Security taxes, and Medicare taxes, and deposit these taxes either monthly or semiweekly.

Social Security and Medicare taxes must be reported and paid separately. Estimated taxes, paid quarterly with Form 1040ES, are generally 25% of the required annual estimated tax.

Federal (FUTA) and state (SUTA) unemployment taxes are used to pay unemployment compensation to employees who have lost their jobs. FUTA is paid only by the employer, quarterly. By January 31, employers must file Form 940 to report annual FUTA payments and deposit any balance due.

State Taxes

A business with employees must also file a Combined Employer's Registration Report (Form 150-211-055) form with the Oregon Department of Revenue to get an Oregon business identification number (BIN). Oregon employers must:

- register for an account with the Oregon Department of Revenue as soon it is known they will have employees.
- withhold state tax from employee wages when they are paid.
- deposit that tax on the same deposit dates as federal withholding tax and FICA tax.
- file combined tax returns in addition to making the required payments.

All employers with open employer accounts must file an Oregon Quarterly Tax Report (OQ), even if they have no payroll during that period.

On the state and local level an employer might have to withhold from employees' wages state withholding tax, state corporate excise tax, state unemployment tax, and workers' compensation premiums, and transit district excise tax, paid to the Tri-County Metropolitan Transportation District (Tri-Met) and the Lane County Mass Transit District (LTD).

Forms and deadlines for filing business income tax returns depend on the type of business:

- An individual proprietor must submit a Schedule C with his individual federal income tax return and use Oregon Form 40 and Schedule SE to report self-employment tax due on net profit.
- A partnership pays no tax, but it must, by the 15th of the fourth month after the end of the fiscal year, submit Form 1065 and Oregon Form 65 to report income from the business. It must report to the partners with Form 1065-K-1. The partners then report that income on Form 1040-Schedule E.
- A corporation must submit federal Form 1120 by the 15th day of the third month after the end of the fiscal year, and use Oregon Form 20 to pay income tax on net profit.
- An S corporation is treated as a partnership and pays no taxes, but it must submit Form 1120-S by the 15th of the third month after the end of the fiscal year.

Payroll Records

Among the records employers must keep are:

- the employer identification number.
- the amounts and dates of all wage, annuity and pension payments.
- the fair market value of in-kind wages paid.
- the names, addresses, Social Security numbers and occupations of employees.
- the dates of employment.
- copies of employees' income tax withholding allowance certificates (Forms W-4, W-4P, W-4S, and W-4V).
- copies of returns filed.
- the records of fringe benefits provided, including substantiation.

Employer Responsibilities

For new employees, employers must verify work eligibility, record names and Social Security numbers from Social Security cards, and ask for Form W-4.

Each payday employers must withhold federal income tax, based on Form W-4, and the employee's share of Social Security and Medicare taxes.

Monthly or semiweekly, they must deposit (less any advance earned income credit):

- withheld income tax.
- withheld and employer Social Security taxes.
- withheld and employer Medicare taxes.

Quarterly (by April 30, July 31, October 31, and January 31), they must:

- deposit FUTA tax in an authorized financial institution if over $100.
- file Form 941 (and pay tax with return if not required to deposit).

Annually, they must:

- ask for a new Form W-4 from employees claiming or changing withholding exemptions.
- reconcile Forms 941 with Forms W-2 and W-3.
- furnish each employee a Form W-2 and each independent contractor a Form 1099 (e.g., Forms 1099-A and 1099-MISC).
- file:
  - o Copy A of Forms W-2 and the transmittal Form W-3 with the SSA.
  - o Forms 1099 and the transmittal Form 1096.
  - o Form 940 or 940EZ.
  - o Form 945 for any nonpayroll income tax withholding.

Brain Teaser

Reinforce your understanding of the material by correctly completing the following sentences:

1. The _____ _____ will generally spell out what is expected of an associate in his day-to-day activities, as well as what the associate can expect of the company.

2. The principal broker must review all transaction documents to ensure that the associate does not act as an agent and an _____ principal in any transaction.

3. A _____ _____ shows the financial condition of the business on a given date.

4. A _____ is a detailed plan of future receipts and expenditures.

5. A business with employees needs to file Form _____ with the IRS to get an employer identification number (EIN).

Brain Teaser Answers

1. The **policy manual** will generally spell out what is expected of an associate in his day-to-day activities, as well as what the associate can expect of the company.

2. The principal broker must review all transaction documents to ensure that the associate does not act as an agent and an **undisclosed** principal in any transaction.

3. A **balance sheet** shows the financial condition of the business on a given date.

4. A **budget** is a detailed plan of future receipts and expenditures.

5. A business with employees needs to file Form **SS-4** with the IRS to get an employer identification number (EIN).

Review – Oregon Manuals and Reports

This lesson provides an overview of the advantages and the format of a good company policies and procedures manual. It also explains two key financial reports, the balance sheet and the income statement, as well as budgets, tax and payroll requirements of a brokerage.

Policies and Procedures
Policies and procedures are standing plans for repetitive action. They are available to cover certain situations whenever they arise.

A policy is a general guide to action. Procedures are specific statements as to what actions are to be taken. A procedure is a standard method of operation, indicating the preferred method of handling the described situation rather than the only method.

Policy Manual
The policy manual is a statement or declaration of the company's policy, philosophy, procedures, and rules and regulations. It will generally spell out what is expected of an associate in his day-to-day activities, as well as what the associate can expect of the company. It should include those items that will make it easier to delegate authority and responsibility and help establish the most economical and effective way of doing certain jobs.

One item required by the Real Estate Agency is a written company policy that sets forth the types of relationships real estate licensees associated with the business may establish. In addition to these required items, many manuals will state the objectives of the company and the expected objectives of its associates.

Manual Uses
The manual helps establish and maintain good relations between associates and between associates and management, so disputes between the parties can be prevented or easily resolved. Where disputes cannot be prevented, it provides grievance procedures. It also makes it easier to recruit new licensees and licensees from other companies and to train new licensees and reinforce policy and procedures for existing licensees. Policies and procedures that are in writing are easier to understand and remember.

A principal broker is responsible under the license law for supervising the personal transactions of his licensees. Principal brokers will establish written company policies relating to personal transactions and include provisions relating to any affiliated licensee compensation in their independent contractor agreements.

Balance Sheet
A balance sheet shows the financial condition of the business on a given date, often at the close of business at the end of a fiscal year, or at the end of a month or a quarter. It sets forth the amounts of the company's assets, liabilities, and capital (also called, net worth

or owner's equity) in two columns. Assets are listed on one side and liabilities and net worth on the other. The total of the assets will equal, or balance, with the total of the liabilities and net worth, creating the basic accounting equation.

An asset is anything of value owned by the business, whether it is owned free and clear or subject to a loan. Assets can be tangible or intangible. They can include such items as prepaid rent, prepaid insurance, land, buildings, equipment, notes and accounts receivable, furniture, fixtures, and the value of a franchise or a franchise name.

On the other side of the balance sheet are liabilities and net worth. Liabilities, or debts, are claims of others to the total assets of the business. They are obligations of the company to pay money or other assets, or to render services, to others, such as taxing authorities, trade suppliers, employees, and financial institutions.

Net worth (or owner's equity) is the difference between the total assets and the total liabilities. Under net worth, the balance sheet may show, as of the beginning of the year, the owner's investment, or the capital stock if it is a corporation, and any additional capital contributions made by the owner to the business during the year.

Income Statement

The income statement (also called a profit and loss statement, an income and expense statement, or an operating statement) shows the company's income and expenses or profit or loss for a given period; often a month, a quarter, or a year. The difference shown on the statement between the company's gross income and its expenses is its net profit or loss for the period.

Budgeting

A budget is a detailed plan of future receipts and expenditures, a projected profit and loss statement, that enables the broker to set a goal and list the steps necessary to reach that goal. Budgeting requires the broker to consider his basic objectives, policies, plans, and resources; ensure his company is properly organized; coordinate with his management team a comprehensive and informative effort to achieve common objectives; and ensure that there are proper companywide controls and procedures.

In a break-even analysis, the broker determines the level of sales necessary to cover costs.

Taxes

A principal broker must promptly pay federal and state taxes and charges for the business and keep complete and accurate records of all business dealings. On the federal level, the broker must withhold from an employee's wages, federal withholding tax and the employee's portion of the Medicare and Social Security premiums; pay federal unemployment tax; and pay an amount matching the employee's share for Social Security tax and Medicare tax.

Oregon Offices and Actions

Overview

In this lesson we discuss the real estate office, the statutory and regulatory requirements for offices, site selection and office layout and equipment. Violations of the license law and the effects of disciplinary actions on a licensee conclude the lesson.

Objectives

Upon completion of this lesson, the student should be able to:

1. Establish a real estate office in compliance with the license law and administrative rules.
2. Describe factors relating to selection of a business location.
3. Discuss considerations for office decor and furnishings.
4. Evaluate various types of office layouts.
5. Identify and describe technology and communication equipment that maximize efficiency.
6. Identify the major grounds for disciplinary action against licensees.
7. Describe types of sanctions that may be imposed on licensees.

Office Setup

Each principal broker, unless a reciprocal broker, must maintain in Oregon a place of business designated as a main office. A person with a reciprocal license must have a place of business in his home state, and cannot have a place of business in Oregon. He can come into the state to engage in transactions, but he cannot work out of an office here.

A licensee's place of business must be specified in the real estate license application and designated in the license. If a licensee does not have an office, he may apply for an inactive license.

Branch Offices

A principal broker may conduct and supervise the business of more than one office, whether it is a main office or a branch office.

A **branch office** is any business location other than the main office:

- where professional real estate activity is regularly conducted, or
- which is advertised as a place where such business may be regularly conducted.

Model units or temporary structures used solely to hand out information and distribute lawfully required public reports are not considered branch offices. However, a booth placed in a shopping mall to display information on listings that is regularly staffed by licensees, would not be a temporary information structure and would need to be registered as a branch office.

A **model unit** is not considered a branch office as long as it is:

- a permanent residential structure located in a subdivision or development;
- used only for distribution and dissemination of information, rather than as a place to transact sales activity; and
- at all times available for sale, lease, lease-option, or exchange. (The broker may have to move his information from one unit to another as the units are sold.)

A principal broker may establish any number of branch offices as separate business locations under his management, provided each is registered with the Real Estate Commissioner. A broker may register a branch office by paying a fee and supplying its street and mailing address to the Commissioner on an Agency-approved form. Registration does not require renewal.

Sign Requirements

A broker's office must have a business **sign** containing the name under which the broker is licensed. A licensee may not display any name as the business name of the company at a designated place of business other than the name under which he is licensed. While the office could be in a broker's home or another place of business, the sign requirement does not authorize the broker to maintain an office or an office sign in conflict with any local zoning regulations, local ordinances, or state laws.

Upon ceasing to engage in professional real estate activity and vacating any business location, the broker must see that his name, or the name under which he has operated, is removed from that location. This means all signs or other identifying information that would show the location as a business location for a real estate broker must be removed.

Office Relocation and Closure

Before changing a business location, a broker must notify the Real Estate Commissioner in writing of the new location. Failure to do so would be grounds for revocation of his license. A principal broker who ceases to maintain a place of business designated as a main office, must return his real estate license to the Real Estate Commissioner. In addition, a principal broker would have to release the licenses of all brokers associated with him.

----- S<small>ITE</small> S<small>ELECTION</small> -----

General Area

A brokerage concentrating on listing and selling residential real estate in suburban locations generally will locate in a commercial area within the area it intends to service.

If possible, the office should be located on a main street, so it reminds people driving by of the broker's presence, or located by a highway exit that will be convenient for the associates to get to and from and will be easy for customers to find. A preferred location would be in the path of local traffic, have adequate parking for associates and clients, and have easy access to roads leading to all parts of the office's service area.

In a smaller town, a residential brokerage may select a major business district that is relatively convenient to all parts of the town or county, close to other businesses and services with which the broker will have to work, visible to the public, and likely to give the company a strong identity within the community, thereby aiding the broker's public relations efforts.

In addition to the downtown area and local business strips, brokers often locate in small shopping centers, offering advantages of signage and on-site parking. They generally avoid the large shopping centers because:

- walk-in visitors they may attract generally are not viable clients or customers.
- the space is expensive, and the expense may not be covered by the business generated from locating in the shopping center.
- a large parking lot is not a convenience if there is no reserved parking.
- there may be sign limitations restricting company exposure.

Many brokers select space near a large center to get sign exposure to the customers of the shopping center, yet avoid the disadvantages of the shopping center itself.

Brokers who deal in specialized types of properties, such as retirement communities or condominiums, may locate branch offices close to areas with large numbers of such properties.

Space in the downtown of a larger city or in a large suburban office complex may be the preference of a broker specializing in commercial, industrial, investment property, or a broker engaged in property management, or a large residential brokerage for his administrative office, even though it will be more expensive and may be less convenient to associates than comparable space in less dense areas.

Office buildings and detached buildings are very attractive to brokers, as they often have ample parking and may provide reserved parking for visitors close to the offices. The few spaces made available should satisfy needs of the office.

In the selection of office space, the broker choosing between ground floor space and upper floor space needs to weigh the additional cost of ground floor space and the convenience to the associates against the walk-in traffic it may promote, which does not usually translate to additional business. Space on an upper floor would be less expensive, and in many cases may provide the benefit of better sign exposure.

Using information concerning growth patterns in an area and other demographic information, the broker can make informed decisions about office location and/or expansion, how much to invest in an expansion, and the size of the facility needed. He can also determine if he can depend on his niche market(s), and estimate a realistic percentage of sales he can expect to capture in the next three to five years.

Governmental, social, and physical boundaries will limit the area that may be conveniently served by an office and the area from which an office may successfully recruit and retain associates.

- Governmental restrictions may form barriers to development in an area.
- Social barriers will prevent people in one locale (whether a neighborhood, suburb, or city) from using an office in the adjacent locale.
- Physical barriers can be manmade or natural. Manmade barriers include such items as highways, shopping malls, bridges, and large buildings. Natural barriers include lakes, rivers, ravines, and mountains.

Branch Offices

The presence or absence of these limiting factors or barriers will affect a broker's decision to open a branch office and his placement of that office. When planning the opening of a new branch office, the broker should consider the location of the branch office in relation to the main office or to another branch in order to avoid doubling his overhead to cover the same area and population. Before opening a branch office, a broker should study the area limits that the existing office is currently serving and compare it to the area to be served by the proposed office.

----- BUY, BUILD OR LEASE -----

The majority of new principal brokers will rent office space. This may range from space that occupies an entire building to a shared facility office where the broker rents a single office in a larger suite and shares a receptionist and other facilities provided by the building management.

The office lease should specify:
- the amount of rent.
- provisions for rental adjustments.
- the lease term.
- renewal and termination provisions.
- the lessor's tenant improvement contributions.
- who is responsible for alterations, repairs, and improvements.
- details of the property insurance held by the landlord and the coverage required of the tenant.
- sublease and assignment restrictions.
- expansion possibilities.
- zoning restrictions.
- tenant remedies in the event use of the premises is interrupted.
- tenant remedies for landlord breach of the lease.
- provisions for dispute resolution.

The ideal lease for the broker would be a long-term lease that would provide ongoing or periodic termination rights or include options to downsize, which would shift part of the risk to the landlord. Often with a long-term lease it is possible to negotiate rent-free occupancy for a number of months. The landlord may offer a short-term lease package with lower concessions, with options to renew, or with enhanced rights to sublet. Before signing a lease, the broker should have an attorney or a colleague experienced in leasing commercial property as well as an experienced insurance agent review the document.

----- THE OFFICE -----

There are many considerations besides cost to take into account when determining the needs of the office. Among the types of issues the broker must consider are:
- the office's design, decor and furnishings.
- the needs of those who use the office.
- the physical layout of the office.

Design, Décor, Furnishings

Design
The architecture of a building can effectively project an image. A broker could choose:

- a colonial-style building to reflect a well-established or conservative firm.
- a contemporary style to project the image of a firm with modern ideas.
- functional space in an office building to just get the job done.

Décor
The style of the office décor and furnishings will also affect the company's profile and image. A broker may choose a progressive style to appeal to younger urban buyers, who may be looking for a residence, a commercial venue, or investment property. A broker may use a city sophisticate style to show a classical inclination and then have the licensees adhere to a dress code to match the office style. A city neighborhood style is for the people who want the "familiar." A suburban residential style suits a brokerage firm that locates and operates in suburban areas, as it adapts its style to its surroundings. Most farm and ranch brokerage firms will want to be welcoming, with comfortable chairs and a work-like environment, but with enough warmth to show that the clients and customers will not be hurried.

Often companies with branch offices try to keep the design and colors of their offices uniform throughout the company in order to establish an easily recognizable identity and keep costs low. If the broker wishes to open a branch office or has to consolidate, with furnishings in all the offices similar, he can move them among locations.

Furnishings
The broker will need to purchase or lease furnishings for the office. Office furniture should be selected with two audiences in mind: the associates and the customers. Associates who work in comfortable surroundings are generally more productive, and more efficient equipment means lower operating costs.

Clients in comfortable surroundings will be more receptive. The persons using a real estate firm want to do business in an environment that is clean, neat, and in good repair. However, expensive furniture and artwork will be a waste of money if they do not help to generate business. If clients rarely come to the office to do business, the broker should not invest heavily in furnishings to impress clients. A broker with a limited budget may rent or lease-purchase, rather than invest in the outright purchase of furniture, in order to give the appearance of an upscale operation.

Among the furniture needed in a brokerage are the following pieces:
- Lobby couch and table
- Conference table and chairs
- Pictures or maps for wall
- Lamps and other adequate lighting
- Rugs
- Wall dividers
- Manager's desk, chair and credenza
- Agent desks and chairs
- Staff desks and chairs
- Workspace shelving for equipment and production
- Filing cabinets to maintain and provide easy access to transaction files
- Fireproof safe to hold essential documents and valuables

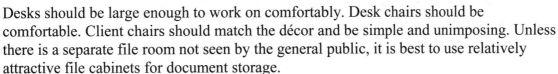

Desks should be large enough to work on comfortably. Desk chairs should be comfortable. Client chairs should match the décor and be simple and unimposing. Unless there is a separate file room not seen by the general public, it is best to use relatively attractive file cabinets for document storage.

The office will end up purchasing an enormous amount of supplies including the following:
- Signs (e.g., firm name, For Sale, Open House, riders)
- Letterhead
- Business cards
- Flyer paper
- Brochure stock
- Reams of white copy paper
- Ink cartridges
- Copier toner
- Normal office supplies (pens, etc.)
- Paper cutter
- Laminator
- Binder

The Needs of Those Who Use the Office

There are a number of factors, in addition to cost, that influence the physical size needs of an office. For a broker who will actually need office space, the following should be considered:
- The number of walk-ins, or clients and customers who have an appointment, that the office may have to assist can vary widely according to the time of year, the

day of the week, or the time of day.
- The office must have a secure place where items can be dropped off or picked up by other visitors the company receives, such as escrow deliveries, vendors, and express mail couriers.
- The number of agents who may occasionally have to use the office computer system should be taken into account as well as the number of agents expected to use the office computer on a daily basis.
- The broker should determine the proportion of sales teams the office has, compared to individual agents.
- There should be sufficient room for the sales staff, employees, and manager to accomplish their work comfortably and efficiently.
- The broker should estimate the number of agents one particular location can accommodate before it would become necessary to expand.

Physical Layout

There are a number of characteristics that are prevalent in most real estate offices. The designated broker and/or the sales manager needs a place to have a private conversation with his employees, licensees, clients, customers, and peers. This can be:
- a private office for his exclusive use.
- an office that doubles as a conference room.
- a conference room that doubles as an office.
- a shared office that can be vacated if the broker needs privacy.

In offices that do not have a conference room, the principal broker may allow an associate to use his office when privacy is required.

Most offices have either a separate waiting room or at least a reception area where visitors can be seated.

There will always be a call for a certain number of private offices. It is increasingly common to have an affiliated licensee pay a fee for the privilege of using one of these offices.

Storage areas are needed for storing required files and records, supplies, signs, and other items necessary to run an office.

A modest office may have a small area set aside for coffee or refreshments. If possible, a break room, which is off-limits to the public, is a welcome addition.

A small meeting space is needed so that agents and their clients can engage in negotiations or discuss private matters, such as financing, and prequalification information. Large meeting space is great to have for occasional meetings, but other arrangements can be made if space is at a premium. If there is a large

conference room, office (sales) meetings can be held there. If there is no large room, brokers will hold the meetings in the open space of the office or at a location outside the office.

Bathroom facilities must be available for the comfort of clients as well as for members of the firm.

Closed-Area Offices
The two most prevalent alternatives for a physical layout for a real estate office are:
- small individual or shared offices, or closed area; and
- a large open community area with separate desks.

An office that provides small offices or cubicles for their associates normally has the offices placed around the perimeter of the office space to take advantage of the windows. The reception area, the work area, and the storage area are in the center portion of the general office.

Advantages to this kind of setup include the following:
- Each associate has a sense of importance
- The client or customer has a sense of dealing with someone of status
- The affiliated licensee and his clients are allowed to have a great deal of privacy
- There is far less noise and distraction
- Agents have an easier time keeping client and customer information confidential

There are some disadvantages to this system, however:
- It is more costly for the brokerage because this is a less efficient use of space than the open design
- The associates can become reclusive, because communication may be eliminated
- Neither the affiliated licensees nor the clients and customers notice the activity going on in the office

Open-Area Office
Many firms use a large open area as the center of activity for their company. In some of these offices, associates have been assigned their own desk. In other offices more than one agent may share desks.

In the open-area environment, the reception area is generally at the front door, and the work area and the storage area are in the back of the open space. The reception area would contain space for filing, answering the telephone, and greeting visitors.

In this arrangement, it is more difficult to keep information confidential. Phone conversations can be overheard. Files cannot be left in or on desks. Therefore, associates working in this type of environment are tempted to take their materials and files home and do more work out of their homes than in the office.

If the office has effective policies for maintaining confidentiality and each associate has his own desk, this arrangement can be an economical way to operate. If the office is active, it can assist in motivating those agents who spend time at the office by allowing them to observe the activity going on around them.

Americans with Disabilities Act

The **Americans with Disabilities Act (ADA)** affects brokers as employers and as providers of commercial services. Title I of the Act provides that businesses with 15 or more employees may not discriminate against an individual with a disability in hiring or promotion if the person is otherwise qualified for the job. A person would be qualified if he meets legitimate skill, experience, education, or other requirements of an employment position that he holds or seeks and can perform the essential functions of the position with or without reasonable accommodation.

Reasonable accommodation might include the following:

- Restructuring the job
- Modifying work schedules
- Acquiring or modifying equipment
- Modifying training materials or policies
- Providing qualified readers or interpreters to blind employees

It also includes modifying the existing facilities used by employees in order to make them readily accessible to and usable by an individual with a disability. Such modifications include the following:

- Reserving accessible and clearly labeled parking spaces
- Creating a level or ramped entrance
- Widening access to conference rooms, restrooms, and cafeterias

The reasonableness portion of this requirement means an employer does not have to lower quality or quantity standards or impose an undue hardship on his business operations in order to make the accommodation. The law applies to real estate firms just as it does to other business entities. Therefore, if a person confined to a wheelchair applied to be an associate with a principal broker, the principal broker could not refuse to hire him on the basis of his confinement. Also, the principal broker would have to provide access for such an associate if modifications may reasonably be made. Such

modifications might include providing assigned parking, widening doorways to allow for passage of the wheelchair and installing ramps at entrances if necessary.

Title III of the Act addresses public accommodations and services in commercial facilities. These are defined as private facilities intended for nonresidential use whose operations will affect commerce. This would include a place of employment, a manufacturing facility, a mall, a retail outlet, an office building, or a real estate office.

The law applies to any private entity that owns, leases, leases to, or operates a place whose operations affect commerce. Therefore, it may apply to the owner, the tenant, the landlord, or an operator of the place used.

A public accommodation is prohibited from discriminating against individuals on the basis of a disability in the full and equal enjoyment of goods, services, facilities, privileges, advantages, and accommodations of any place of public accommodation. It must provide the opportunity for disabled persons to participate in the services or goods of its business on an equal basis with nondisabled persons. To do this, it may need to:

- modify its business practices where such modifications would not fundamentally alter the nature of the service or business.
- remove architectural barriers where removal is readily achievable.

New construction must be designed to be readily accessible to persons with disabilities unless it would be structurally impracticable to do so. Readily accessible means that individuals with disabilities can approach, enter, and use the facility easily and conveniently.

All alterations to existing commercial facilities and public accommodations must, to the maximum extent feasible, be made in a manner readily accessible to disabled individuals. An alteration is a change to the facility that affects or could affect the usability of the building or facility or any part of it, such as remodeling, renovation, restoration, and changes or rearrangements in structural parts or elements.

----- TECHNOLOGY AND COMMUNICATION EQUIPMENT -----

Generally, a real estate office will need a copy machine, a fax machine, a number of computers, and high-speed access to the Internet. The office will also require a phone system with several lines. For associates, the principal broker needs sufficient tables or desks that have room for a computer, monitor, and phone. Office machinery and equipment can be standardized throughout all offices.

The principal broker will want to have one or more computers in the office, either networked (connected to one another) or as stand-alone units. The computers should have a large-capacity hard drive, because most real estate practitioners end up with many programs and take a lot of photographs, which take up a lot of space on the hard drive.

A certain portion of the office equipment should be provided by the brokerage for use of the principal broker, management, staff, and licensees. Some managers will charge for use of services such as photocopies. Others absorb the cost as a business expense covered by the desk fee or the brokerage portion of the commission split they take from the agents.

A large, flat-screen monitor will help to ease eyestrain and allows the user to keep multiple files open on the computer screen simultaneously. If possible, the broker should get an ergonomic, wireless keyboard, and a wireless, optical mouse. DVD-RW (read and write) high-capacity removable disk players come standard on most computers today. A broker should consider removable storage that comes in a size no larger than a tube of lipstick.

There are a variety of printers available to satisfy different needs. Full-color laser printers are not cost prohibitive anymore, although inkjet printers are fine for economical black-and-white or color prints. A label printer comes in handy if promotional materials are sent out.

Most companies will purchase, or at least lease, a relatively fast, efficient stand-alone photocopy machine. A color copier will allow brochures to be produced in-house, at a savings over sending material out to be printed. There are also printers that can produce an inordinate amount of flyers, brochures, and other documents as quickly as a photocopier. When acquiring one or both of these machines, whether by lease or by purchase, the broker should investigate the cost of toner cartridges and how many documents are produced per cartridge, so he can project a per-copy cost.

Scanners allow a person to:
- scan a document with a signature and send it to another person via the Internet.
- scan documents into memory.
- with OCR (Optical Character Recognition) software, scan documents into a program and then change the document.

Mini-scanners enter business cards into memory and have the capability of recognizing which data is a phone number, which is an address, and which is the person's name and title. Printer-copier-scanner all-in-one machines are readily available; unfortunately, when one part malfunctions, they all malfunction.

Every office will have a fax machine, even if it is sitting on a shelf and needs to be plugged into the phone cord. When necessary, it can serve as a copier. Many computers also have facsimile capabilities, and if the computer is attached to high-speed Internet access, there is no need to take up a phone line in order to send a fax.
Available software programs can help real estate professionals perform their everyday activities. Some software comes with a huge number of preformatted brochures, clip art, photographic enhancement, and other capabilities. Graphic design programs and CAD (computer-assisted design) programs enable agents to prepare anything from brochures and flyers to the blueprints of a building, including landscaping.

Violations of License Law

----- VIOLATIONS -----

Section 696.301 of the license law authorizes the Real Estate Commissioner to suspend or revoke the real estate license of any real estate licensee, reprimand any licensee or deny the issuance or renewal of a license to an applicant who has done any of the following:

- Created a reasonable probability of damage or injury to a person by making one or more material misrepresentations or false promises in a matter related to professional real estate activity (This might include making an intentional misrepresentation or false promise to a purchaser, even though the purchaser did not buy the property and even though his client approved of the misrepresentation; making a misrepresentation by omission; or promising or guaranteeing, or authorizing an associate to guarantee, future profits on the resale of real property.)
- Knowingly or recklessly published materially misleading or untruthful advertising
- Represented, attempted to represent or accepted a commission or other compensation from a principal broker other than the principal broker with whom the broker is associated
- Disregarded or violated any provision of the state fair housing law or the real estate license law, or any rule of the Agency, or any term, condition, restriction or limitation contained in an order issued by the Commissioner (This might include:
  - o engaging in blockbusting or steering.
  - o failing to give a buyer a copy of his offer before submitting it to the seller.
  - o failing to mention the type of earnest money in the sales agreement.
  - o failing to deliver a completed copy of an offer to the buyer or seller within a reasonable time.
  - o advertising property or placing a For Sale sign on it without the written consent of the owner.
  - o conducting property management activity in the name of the associate, instead of in the name of the principal broker.
  - o receiving compensation from any person in a real estate transaction, such as a bonus from a seller, other than his principal broker.
  - o paying a finder's fee to an unlicensed person.
  - o any violation of the agency provisions of the license law, such as failing to submit all written offers from or to a client, quoting prices other than authorized by a client, and acting for more than one party in a transaction without the knowledge and written permission of both.)
- Acted as an agent and an undisclosed principal in any transaction

- Accepted employment or compensation for the preparation of a competitive market analysis or letter opinion that is contingent upon reporting a predetermined value or for real estate in which the licensee had an undisclosed interest
- Represented a taxpayer contingent upon reporting a predetermined value or for real estate in which the licensee had an undisclosed interest
- Failed to ensure, in any real estate transaction in which the licensee performed the closing, that the buyer and seller received a complete detailed closing statement showing the amount and purpose of all receipts, adjustments and disbursements
- Has been convicted of a felony or misdemeanor substantially related to his trustworthiness or competence to engage in professional real estate activity
- Committed an act of fraud or engaged in dishonest conduct substantially related to his fitness to conduct professional real estate activity, without regard to whether the act or conduct occurred in the course of professional real estate activity
- Demonstrated incompetence or untrustworthiness in performing any act for which the licensee is required to hold a license
- Engaged in any conduct that is below the standard of care for the practice of professional real estate activity in Oregon as established by the community of persons engaged in the practice of professional real estate activity in Oregon
- Intentionally interfered with the contractual relations of others concerning real estate or professional real estate activity or with the exclusive representation or exclusive brokerage relationship of another licensee

----- ENFORCEMENT -----

In administering the law, the Agency will audit real estate offices, investigate matters reported by licensees and respond to complaints from consumers.

Brokerage firms are randomly selected for **audits** to ascertain that their trust accounts are in proper order and that their standards of operation meet all legislative and administrative requirements.

Adverse Decisions
The Agency will also investigate matters reported by licensees. A licensee must notify the Commissioner of the following:
- Any criminal conviction (felony or misdemeanor), including a "no contest" plea or bail forfeiture
- Any adverse decision or judgment resulting from any civil or criminal suit or action, arbitration proceeding or administrative or Oregon State Bar proceeding related to him:
  - in which he was named as a party; and
  - against whom allegations concerning any business conduct or professional real estate activity is asserted

- Any adverse decision or judgment resulting from any other criminal or civil proceeding that reflects adversely on the "trustworthy and competent" requirements in the statute and rules

The required notification must be in writing and include:
- a brief description of the circumstances involved.
- the names of the parties.
- a copy of the adverse decision, judgment, or award and, in the case of a criminal conviction, a copy of the sentencing order.

This notification must be made within 20 calendar days after receipt of written notification of an adverse judgment, award, or decision, rule whether or not the decision is appealed. If the judgment, award, or decision is appealed, each subsequent appellate court decision must be reported even if it is not adverse. The licensee is not permitted to delay reporting until all appeals have been concluded.

The licensee is not required to notify the Commissioner of:
- any administrative proceeding determination of the Agency.
- arbitration proceedings between licensees concerning only a commission payment dispute.
- adverse rulings or settlements where the licensee is the claimant and suffers an adverse decision.

Complaints and Investigations

In the event of a **complaint** against a licensee that alleges ground for discipline, the Commissioner and his staff can use investigative subpoenas to gather information from the complainants, witnesses and real estate licensees alike.

The Commissioner or an Agency manager will review the complaint to determine whether there are reasonable grounds to believe that a violation of the license law or administrative rules may have occurred that constitutes grounds for discipline.

Reasonable grounds means a reasonable belief in facts or circumstances which, if true, would constitute such a violation. If it is determined that there are reasonable grounds to believe a violation may have occurred, the Agency will initiate an investigation.

The individual assigned to investigate the complaint will:
- gather all relevant facts in an objective, impartial and unbiased manner. He may electronically record an investigative interview if the person to be interviewed states his consent to the recording on the recording.
- issue a report containing all facts discovered during the investigation, including those that may be exculpatory or mitigating.
- promptly notify the Commissioner or an Agency manager if a licensee fails or refuses to cooperate in an investigation.

- not communicate with a licensee or a member of the public about:
  o the findings of the investigation.
  o whether a violation may have occurred based on the facts.
  o whether the Agency will initiate administrative action against him.
- not solicit complaints against any licensee.
- limit the scope of the investigation to the conduct or transaction(s) that formed the basis for initiating the investigation. However, if there are reasonable grounds to believe that additional violations may have occurred that would result in reprimand, suspension, revocation or license denial, the Commissioner or an Agency manager may expand the scope of the investigation or authorize additional investigations.
- write the investigation report in an objective manner and not include any conclusions about whether a violation has occurred or any recommendation regarding discipline.

An Agency manager will review the investigation report and file and determine whether the evidence supports charging a person under investigation with a violation of the license law or rules. The Agency will not assert, propose to stipulate to, or issue a contested case notice alleging a violation of the statutes and rules without reasonable grounds.

In addition, the Commissioner's investigative staff is able to subpoena records and require testimony in administrative hearings. Failure to comply with a subpoena may result in civil penalty or confinement in

Sanctions
If a license applicant does not disclose a prior criminal history or is not, in general, trustworthy for issuance of a license, the Commissioner may deny issuance of the

requested license, or he may issue a **probationary license**, requiring satisfaction of specified conditions prior to obtaining a regular license. The conditions often include requiring the principal broker to submit progress reports and to maintain close supervision of his licensee. Also, the applicant cannot have any new criminal arrests or convictions. Violation of these license conditions may result in the immediate loss of the probationary license.

Any real estate licensee who disregards or violates any provision of the license law, the Agency's rules, or the state statute against discrimination is subject to disciplinary action by the Commissioner. If the licensee fails to comply with the law or the administrative rules and regulations related to real estate brokers, the Commissioner may formally reprimand him, suspend his license, revoke his license, or deny renewal of the license. In addition, a licensee may be assessed a civil penalty if he conducts professional real estate activity while his license is on inactive status or suspended, or after his license has expired or been revoked.

The fact that a license has lapsed, is suspended or has been surrendered will not deprive the Commissioner of jurisdiction to proceed with any investigation, action or disciplinary proceedings relating to the licensee, or to revise or void an order suspending or revoking the license.

Progressive Discipline

The law and Agency rules provide for progressive discipline. **Progressive discipline** is a process the Agency follows, which uses increasingly severe steps or measures against a licensee who fails to correct inappropriate behavior or exhibits further instances of inappropriate behavior.

The goal of progressive discipline is to:
- correct a licensee's inappropriate behavior.
- deter the licensee from repeating the conduct.
- educate the licensee to improve compliance with applicable statutes and rules.

Before determining whether to issue a non-disciplinary educational letter of advice or to discipline a licensee through reprimand, suspension or revocation, the Commissioner will evaluate all relevant factors, including:
- the nature of the violation.
- the harm caused, if any.
- whether the conduct was inadvertent or intentional.
- the licensee's experience and education.
- whether the licensee's conduct is substantially similar to conduct or an act for which he was disciplined previously.
- any mitigating or aggravating circumstances.
- the licensee's cooperation with the investigation.
- any Agency hearing orders addressing similar circumstances.
- the licensee's volume of transactions.

The Commissioner may suspend or revoke a license only if the licensee has committed an act that constitutes grounds for discipline, and:
- results in significant damage or injury;
- exhibits incompetence, dishonesty or fraudulent conduct; or
- repeats conduct or an act substantially similar to that for which he was disciplined previously.

Educational Letter of Advice

If the Commissioner determines that a licensee's conduct is a matter of concern but does not merit disciplinary action, he may issue a non-disciplinary educational letter of advice to the licensee. This letter includes the following statements:
- The Commissioner has determined not to pursue disciplinary action against the licensee
- The letter is the result of an investigation and closes the investigation

- The letter is not disciplinary in nature and will not appear in the agency's disciplinary records
- The purpose of the letter is to educate the licensee
- The letter will be removed from the Agency's records six years from the date of issuance

Reprimand

A **reprimand** is the least formal penalty that may be imposed by the Commissioner. However, it is also the maximum disciplinary action the Commissioner may issue against a licensee who has committed an act or conduct that constitutes grounds for discipline, but does not:

- result in significant damage or injury.
- exhibit incompetence in the performance of professional real estate activity.
- exhibit dishonesty or fraudulent conduct.
- repeat conduct or an act that is substantially similar to that for which he was disciplined previously.

The reprimand is a formal notice to the licensee that he has acted improperly. It does not affect his ability to continue to conduct professional real estate activity, but it is noted on his license history, to ensure that, in the event the same violation is repeated, the Commissioner would have grounds to impose a more severe penalty.

Suspension

A license **suspension** is more severe. It suspends the right to conduct professional real estate activity for a specified period of time (usually ranging from 30 to 90 days). An unexpired real estate license that has been suspended by order of the Commissioner may be reissued upon request and payment of a $10 fee within 30 days after the close of the suspension period. The reissued license is effective the first business day after all required fees and forms are received in the Agency's office. If the licensee does not request reissuance within the 30-day period, he may reactivate the license only by applying for reactivation and paying the $75 reactivation fee. If the license expires during the suspension period or prior to the request for reissuance, it may be renewed only by the licensee satisfying the regular requirements for renewal.

Revocation

License **revocation** is the most severe penalty the Commissioner can impose. It permanently terminates all rights to engage in professional real estate activity in Oregon.

If a license is revoked, it is possible to later reapply for a license as a new applicant. If at the time of application, the applicant qualifies for the license and shows that he is now trustworthy, he could be issued a new license. A licensee cannot knowingly permit a person whose license is suspended or revoked to engage in professional real estate activity with him or on his behalf.

James Wilson, a broker licensed in Oregon, cannot enter into a cooperative transaction with John Weber when he knows that Weber's broker license has been suspended or revoked.

In the event the Agency suspends or revokes a principal broker's license, the licenses of the principal broker's associated licensees are automatically rendered inactive. However, a new license may be issued, if requested within 30 days after the effective date of the suspension or revocation of the principal broker's license, upon payment of the $10 transfer fee.

If the license of the principal broker representing a corporate real estate brokerage is suspended or revoked and the company does not replace the principal broker prior to the effective date of the suspension or revocation, licenses of the licensees in the company will be rendered inactive until the principal broker is changed or until the licensees apply for and are issued new licenses with new principal brokers.

Limited License

At the Commissioner's sole discretion he may issue a **limited license**. Such a license may be limited in any of the following ways:
- Limit the licensee to serve as the agent of a particular principal real estate broker, if the Commissioner feels the licensee received poor supervision from the previous principal broker but would be able to perform acceptably under the supervision of another principal broker
- Have a limited term, allowing the licensee to work for a limited time
- Have conditions to be observed in the exercise of his license and the privileges granted, (e.g., limiting the licensee to residential property transactions, not allowing the licensee to manage properties or to accept or handle funds)

The holder of a limited license does not have any property right in the privileges granted under the license and does not even have the right to renew the license. Renewal would be at the discretion of the Agency. Furthermore, the Commissioner may suspend or revoke the license or reprimand the licensee if the licensee violates the law or any of the terms or conditions contained in the order granting the license.

Failure to Meet Financial Obligations

The Commissioner may also deny issuance of new license or suspend an existing license of any person who has:
- failed or refused to pay a state-guaranteed loan where his default has required the state to pay off the loan.
- pay child support in accordance with a court order or agreement with a District Attorney.
- make any agreed-upon payments of state taxes.

Actions with No Hearing

The Commissioner may take licensing action without an administrative hearing if he determines that the licensee's continued operations pose a substantial threat to his potential customers and clients, such as when the licensee has misappropriated his clients' trust funds or there is a substantial shortage in his clients' trust account. Following issuance of an immediate suspension order, the licensee may request and receive an administrative hearing to contest the order.

When the Commissioner determines that a licensee has commingled trust funds with personal funds or has embezzled trust funds and is likely to cause significant financial loss to others, he may ask the state Attorney General to assist in taking legal action to have a receiver appointed in order to prevent or minimize financial loss to others.

If the Circuit Court is satisfied that receivership is warranted, it will issue an order for a hearing on the matter and may also issue a temporary order, restraining the licensee or any of his officers, directors, stockholders, members, agents or employees from transacting professional real estate activity or wasting or disposing of assets until further order of court.

A hearing on whether the injunction is to be continued then is held within five business days of service of the injunction.

Fines

The Commissioner has authority to impose civil penalties (or fines) against persons who perform professional real estate activity in Oregon without an active real estate license. The fine for the first offense of unlicensed professional real estate activity is $100 to $500. For additional offenses, the fine is $500 to $1,000 per offense. In addition, the Commissioner may impose a civil penalty of up to the amount by which the unlicensed person profited in the transaction. On the other hand, if a licensee conducts professional real estate activity during a period in which his license has expired, all activity conducted within an individual 30-day period thereafter will be inclusive and constitute only one offense per period. Additionally, the licensee is not subject to the per-offense penalty amounts set forth in the law or the civil penalty related to profiting from a transaction.

Criminal Penalties

In addition to all these actions, a violation of any license law provision is a Class A misdemeanor, subject to fine of $5,000 and/or one year in jail. Any officer, director, shareholder, member, or agent of a real estate organization who personally participated in or is an accessory to any violation of the law by his organization is subject to penalties for a Class A misdemeanor.

----- ETHICS -----

The Realtor Code of Ethics which was first written in 1913 before license laws existed has been revised many times over the years and sets forth standards of conduct and professional integrity that are the hallmarks of the real estate profession. While members of the National Association of Realtors are required to adhere to these principles, many non-realtors use them in training session with their agents on real estate ethics. The Code has been held by the courts to contain the standards by which all real estate licenses are held to. To meet their obligations to clients, customers, the public and each other Realtors pledge to:

- protect the individual right of real estate ownership.
- be honorable and honest in all dealings.
- provide superior representation of clients through increased education.
- act fairly toward all in the spirit of the Golden Rule.
- serve well the community and country.
- observe the Realtor's Code of Ethics and conform conduct to its aspirational ideals.

While many sections of the Code mirror Oregon statutes and administrative rules, such as Article 1 which requires a Realtor to "pledge themselves to protect and promote the interests of their clients", others such as the Code requirement that Realtors "shall not undertake to provide specialized professional services concerning a type of property or service that is outside of their field of competence unless they engage the assistance of one who is competent..." Many principal brokers make it a point to periodically review sections of the Code with their associated licensees.

Brain Teaser

Reinforce your understanding of the material by correctly completing the following sentences:

1. A _____ office is any business location other than the main office in which professional real estate activity is regularly conducted.

2. Americans with Disabilities Act (ADA) affects brokers with _____ or more employees.

3. New construction must be designed to be _____ _____ to persons with disabilities unless it would be structurally impracticable to do so.

4. A _____ is the least formal penalty that may be imposed by the Commissioner.

5. License _____ permanently terminates all rights to engage in professional real estate activity in Oregon.

Brain Teaser Answers

1. A **branch** office is any business location other than the main office in which professional real estate activity is regularly conducted.

2. Americans with Disabilities Act (ADA) affects brokers with **15** or more employees.

3. New construction must be designed to be **readily accessible** to persons with disabilities unless it would be structurally impracticable to do so.

4. A **reprimand** is the least formal penalty that may be imposed by the Commissioner.

5. License **revocation** permanently terminates all rights to engage in professional real estate activity in Oregon.

Review – Oregon Offices and Actions

In this lesson we discuss the real estate office, violations of the license law and the effects of disciplinary actions on licensees.

Offices

All brokers, except for reciprocal brokers and brokers associated with a principal real estate broker, must maintain in Oregon a place of business designated as their main office. The place of business must be specified in the real estate license application and designated in the license. If a licensee does not have an office, he may apply for an inactive license.

A or principal broker may establish any number of branch offices, provided each is registered with the Real Estate Commissioner. However, model units or temporary structures used solely to hand out information and distribute lawfully required public reports are not considered branch offices.

A broker's office must have a business sign containing the name under which the broker is licensed. A licensee may not display any name as the business name of the company at a designated place of business other than the name under which he is licensed.

Using information concerning growth patterns in an area and other demographic information, the broker can make informed decisions about office location and/or expansion, how much to invest in an expansion, and the size of the facility needed. He can also determine if he can depend on his niche market(s), and estimate a realistic percentage of sales he can expect to capture in the next three to five years.

Governmental, social, and physical boundaries will limit the area that may be conveniently served by an office and the area from which an office may successfully recruit and retain associates.

There are many considerations besides cost to take into account when determining the needs of the office. Among the types of issues the broker must consider are the office's design, décor and furnishings; the needs of those who use the office; and the physical layout of the office. Office furniture should be selected with two audiences in mind: the associates and the customers.

There are a number of characteristics that are prevalent in most real estate offices. The principal broker and/or the sales manager needs a place to have a private conversation with his employees, licensees, clients, customers, and peers. Most offices have either a separate waiting room or at least a reception area where visitors can be seated. There will always be a call for a certain number of private offices. Storage areas are needed for storing required files and records, supplies, signs, and other items necessary to run an office.

A small meeting space is needed so that agents and their clients can engage in negotiations or discuss private matters, such as financing and prequalification information. Large meeting space is great to have for occasional meetings, but other arrangements can be made if space is at a premium.

Bathroom facilities must be available for the comfort of clients as well as for members of the firm.

The two most prevalent alternatives for a physical layout for a real estate office are small individual or shared offices, or closed area; and a large open community area with separate desks.

Actions

A licensee must notify the Commissioner in writing within 20 days of any adverse decision, judgment or award resulting from any legal proceeding, civil or criminal, or any administrative or Oregon State Bar proceeding in which he was named as a party and against whom allegations concerning his professional real estate activity on his own account or on behalf of others is asserted.

If a licensee fails to comply with the law or the administrative rules and regulations related to real estate brokers, the Commissioner may formally reprimand him, suspend his license, revoke his license, or deny renewal of the license. In addition, any person may be assessed a civil penalty if he conducts professional real estate activity without an active license.

A reprimand is a formal notice to the licensee that he has acted improperly. A license suspension suspends the right to conduct professional real estate activity for a specified period of time. License revocation permanently terminates all rights to engage in professional real estate activity in Oregon. In the event the Agency suspends or revokes a principal broker's license, the licenses of the principal broker's associated licensees are automatically rendered inactive.

A license may be suspended or denied renewal if the licensee failed or refused to pay a state-guaranteed loan where his default has required the state to pay off the loan; pay child support in accordance with a court order or agreement with a District Attorney; or make any agreed-upon payments of state taxes.

Licensing action can be taken without an administrative hearing if the licensee's continued operations pose a substantial threat to his potential customers and clients, such as when he has misappropriated his clients' trust funds or there is a substantial shortage in his clients' trust account.

Oregon Trust Accounts

Overview

This lesson looks at the basics behind trust accounts. It covers principal broker responsibility for trust funds. The handling of earnest money, including deposit, refund, disbursal to escrow, and distribution of forfeited deposits is covered. Requirements for opening and maintaining various types of trust accounts are discussed. Recordkeeping requirements conclude the lesson.

Objectives

Upon completion of this lesson, the student should be able to:

1. Explain the responsibility of licensees with regard to clients' funds.
2. Describe the purpose of a principal broker's trust account.
3. Describe the procedure for opening a trust account.
4. Explain requirements for depositing funds into interest-bearing accounts and depositing funds into escrow accounts.
5. Explain trust account reconciliation.
6. Explain trust account recordkeeping requirements.

Requirements

----- REQUIREMENTS -----

General Checking Account

Every principal broker will keep a **general checking account**. A general account is his operating account, to handle funds that belong to the brokerage firm. Into this account he deposits company income, and from this account he pays all company expenses.

Commissions from sales and/or property management activity are deposited into this account. Fees earned are also deposited into this account. These may include fees collected for competitive market analyses, retainer fees, consulting fees, and fees for other services provided on a "fee for service" basis. This account will contain any funds the principal broker may personally deposit to help pay expenses. This account could also contain rents and other income earned from properties owned by the principal broker, provided they are not under the management of the brokerage.

At no time can any funds belonging to clients or customers be placed into this account. Therefore, if the principal broker's own properties are managed by the company, the principal broker would be considered a client of the company, and he would not be allowed to deposit any rents or other income earned from those properties directly into this account.

Clients' Trust Account

Unless a principal broker always places trust funds from transactions involving the sale, purchase, lease option or exchange of real property in a neutral escrow depository, he must maintain in Oregon at least one separate bank account designated as a **clients' trust account**. A trust account is a bank checking account or an interest-bearing savings account into which the principal broker must deposit all funds received or handled by him or his affiliated licensees on behalf of any other person, except for those funds immediately placed in escrow.

The principal broker must place trust funds into a clients' trust account unless all parties to the transaction agree to deposit the funds in a licensed neutral escrow depository in Oregon. (ORS 696.210)

Trust funds are money or things of value received by the principal broker, or persons associated with the principal broker, on behalf of a principal, or any other person, in performing any professional real estate activity, for which a real estate license is required. The funds do not belong to the principal broker but are being held for the benefit of others. Trust funds include cash, a check or note made payable to the principal broker, a check made payable to an escrow company or title company, a note made payable to the seller, or a registration slip to an automobile being used as a down payment. The principal broker must, as trustee, hold the funds in trust for a buyer and seller, or landlord and tenant, until it has been determined to whom the money belongs.

Notice to Bank

At the time he opens a clients' trust account, the principal broker must notify the bank at which he maintains the account in writing that the account is a clients' trust account for the purpose of holding funds belonging to others, have a bank official sign an acknowledgment of receipt of the notice, and keep an acknowledged copy of the notice in the principal broker's records. The term **bank** does not refer to only a bank. It includes any bank or trust company, savings bank, mutual savings bank, savings and loan association or credit union that maintains a head office or a branch in Oregon and which operates in the capacity of a financial institution.

NOTICE OF CLIENTS' TRUST ACCOUNT

To: (name of bank)

_____

Under the Oregon Real Estate License Law, I am the principal real estate broker or real estate property manager (licensed name of broker or business)

_____.

Further, under ORS 696.241, I am required to maintain in Oregon a Clients' Trust Account for the purpose of holding funds belonging to others.

With regard to the account(s) numbered _____ which is/are designated as a Clients' Trust Account, the account(s) is/are maintained with you as a depository for money belonging to persons other than myself and in my fiduciary capacity as a principal real estate broker established by client agreements in separate documents.

Dated: _____
(insert date)

_____
(signature of property manager)

ACKNOWLEDGMENT OF RECEIPT

I, _____, a duly authorized representative of (bank)
_____, do hereby acknowledge receipt of the above
NOTICE OF CLIENTS' TRUST ACCOUNT on (date)_____.

_____
(signature)

_____
(title)

Various Accounts

A principal broker may have any number of clients' trust accounts. He may have a separate clients' trust account for each branch office. If a branch office does maintain a separate clients' trust account, it must also maintain a separate bookkeeping system in the branch office. Where separate general business and/or trust accounts are maintained at the branch office, financial records may be maintained and located either at the main office or the branch office. If the principal broker engages in property management activities, he must set up separate trust accounts for property management and security deposits.

A principal broker may place trust funds in an interest-bearing bank account, if it is federally insured and designated a clients' trust account and if he has the prior written authorization of all parties having an interest in the trust funds. Therefore, to place an earnest money deposit in an interest-bearing account, he must get written approval from the buyer and the seller. The written approval must be given before the trust funds are deposited and must specify to whom and under what circumstances the interest earnings from the account will accrue and be paid. With the written consent of all parties, interest accrued on the interest-bearing clients' trust account may be paid to the seller, the purchaser or even the principal broker.

Money belonging to others cannot be invested in any type of account, security or certificate of deposit which has a fixed term for maturity or imposes a fee or penalty for withdrawal prior to maturity, unless all parties give written consent. In this case, the principal broker may make an arrangement with the depository to deposit enough of his own funds to maintain the account, without being considered to be commingling.

Notice to Real Estate Agency

The principal broker must notify the Real Estate Agency within 10 days upon opening or closing any clients' trust account. The Agency will want the name of the bank, the account number, and the name of the account for each client's trust account he maintains. The Commissioner must also be provided with authorization to examine the trust accounts. All of this can be done by the principal broker logging in to e-License under their personal license account.

REAL ESTATE AGENCY SCHEDULE OF
1177 CENTER STREET NE TRUST ACCOUNTS
SALEM, OREGON 97310-2503 MAINTAINED
PHONE (503) 378-4170 BY LICENSEE
FAX (503) 373-7153

_____   _____
Licensed Name of Property Manager   Date

_____
Principal Office Address   - or -

_____
Branch Office

CLIENTS' TRUST ACCOUNTS:

Bank Name and Address   Account Number   Account Name
_____   _____   _____
_____   _____   _____
_____   _____   _____
_____   _____   _____
_____   _____   _____

I hereby certify that the above-described bank accounts are all of the trust accounts maintained by this firm. The Real Estate Commissioner shall be notified in writing of any changes to any of the above information.

Authorized Signature

PER ORS 696.241(2) (REAL ESTATE) AND ORS 696.578(2) (ESCROW), THE ABOVE INFORMATION IS TO BE FILED WITH THE REAL ESTATE AGENCY, 1177 CENTER STREET, N.E., SALEM, OREGON 97310.

Authorization to Examine

The principal broker must also authorize the Real Estate Agency to examine the clients' trust accounts at any time the Commissioner may direct such an examination.

REAL ESTATE AGENCY   AUTHORIZATION TO
1177 CENTER STREET NE   EXAMINE CLIENTS'
SALEM, OREGON 97310-2503   TRUST ACCOUNT
PHONE (503) 378-4170
FAX (503) 373-7153

Bank Name   Date

Name of Licensed Firm or Individual

Address   Phone

You are hereby authorized to furnish information requested by the Real Estate Commissioner and/or authorized representative concerning the following client trust account(s):

Account Name   Account No.

NOTE: The Real Estate Commissioner shall be notified by the licensee immediately, by written notice, if any new trust accounts are opened, existing accounts closed, or if any changes in present accounts occur.

Property Manager

(Please Print or Type) Signature

(Please Print or Type) Signature

(Please Print or Type) Signature

(Please Print or Type) Signature

PER ORS 696.241(3) (REAL ESTATE) AND ORS 696.578(2) (ESCROW), THE ABOVE INFORMATION IS TO BE FILED WITH THE REAL ESTATE AGENCY, 1177 CENTER STREET, N.E., SALEM, OREGON 97310.

The Commissioner may have a representative examine the account at any time. Generally, these examinations or audits help to prevent or correct problems before the principal broker gets into trouble. Every principal broker may be visited by an Agency field examiner, who has been assigned by the Commissioner to make a routine office inspection. The examiner will expect to examine all pending real estate transactions and determine amounts and dates of earnest money receipts and disbursements. He will examine the authority for a disbursement, contact the bank where the clients' trust account is located to determine the balance on hand, and audit the account to see that the balance equals the liability. Lack of complete records is considered a serious violation and may prompt a more complete investigation by the Commissioner.

Mail-in Audits

The Real Estate Agency conducts quarterly random mail-in audits of client's trust accounts. Every quarter, 100 client's trust accounts are randomly selected from the Agency's database for audit. All companies maintaining client's trust accounts are likely to be selected for audit. After the audit selection has been made, the Agency sends out letters requesting a copy of the most recent reconciliation and all supporting documentation. In instances where a response is not received within the time period required in the notice, the Agency may initiate an investigation.

There is no requirement that a principal broker notify clients of the name of the bank in which he deposits trust funds or of the trust fund account number.

----- COMMINGLING -----

Clients' funds must be placed in a clients' trust account or neutral escrow depository in order to assure there is no commingling of licensee funds with client funds. **Commingling**, combining a principal broker's personal funds with those of a client, is illegal according to the license law and Real Estate Agency administrative rules. It could occur by placing clients' funds in the principal broker's personal or business account, or by placing the principal broker's business or personal funds, such as earned commissions, in a clients' trust account.

In general, a principal broker may not knowingly keep or cause to be kept any funds or money in any bank under the heading of clients' trust account, or any other name designating the funds or money as belonging to his clients, except actual trust funds deposited with him.

A principal broker who accepts a credit card payment as funds in a real estate transaction must maintain, use and, if necessary, refund, the face amount of the payment without reducing it by any merchant's discount or processing fee unless he has a separate written agreement signed by the credit card user authorizing the discount or fee to be deducted. However, if a refund is necessary, the full face amount, including any discount or fees paid by the credit card, must be refunded to the user.

In no instance may:
- the principal broker benefit from any merchant's discounts or processing fees generated by the use of the credit card.

- the trust account be charged or debited for any merchant's discount or processing fees for use of the credit card in a transaction.

If a principal broker is to be paid a fee or commission from funds in the account (e.g., earnest money or rents) or be paid interest earned in the account as part of his fee or commission, he is not entitled to that money until the transaction has been completed or terminated, and until then that money is not considered commingling of trust funds with his personal funds. Once the transaction has been completed, he should transfer any earned commission to his general operating account promptly, at least within 30 days of when it is earned. The principal broker cannot pay his personal obligations, such as office rent, electricity charges or commissions owed to associates or cooperating principal brokers, out of a trust account, even if they are drawn against earned commissions. Instead, he must transfer his entire commission from the clients' trust account to his general account and write all expense checks from that account.

Also, a principal broker is required to place funds in the clients' trust account or escrow relating to the sale of property owned by himself or owned by licensees working for him in order to protect parties dealing with the licensee. Therefore, earnest money received for the sale of licensee-owned property may be deposited in a clients' trust account.

This requirement does not apply to rental transactions of licensee-owned property, unless the brokerage is managing the property and charging a fee for bookkeeping, management or collection of funds. Therefore, rental collections on licensee-owned property would be placed in the licensee's personal account and not in the clients' trust account.

Also, deferred commission payments and contract collection payments on property where the licensee was the owner-seller are considered personal funds and, therefore, not deposited into the trust account.

Because the principal broker's personal and business funds are kept out of the clients' trust account, funds in the trust account are not subject to execution or attachment on any claim against the principal broker and will not be frozen during probate or other legal proceedings if he were to become incapacitated or die.

Furthermore, when the account is specifically designated as custodial and the name and interest of each owner in the deposit is disclosed on the principal broker's records, funds of all owners placed in the trust account are recognized for deposit insurance purposes to the same extent as if their names and interest were disclosed on the bank's records. The **Federal Deposit Insurance Corporation (FDIC)** insures accounts for up to $250,000 each. When there is a separate ledger for each client, the FDIC will apply this limit to each client rather than to the total of all funds in the trust account. As a result, if a principal broker had $5,000,000 in a trust account, all of the clients with less than $250,000 in that bank would be fully insured. Without a separate accounting of each individual client's funds, the FDIC would insure only $250,000 of the $5,000,000 account.

----- DEPOSITS -----

All trust funds received or handled by the principal broker, or by any licensee associated with him, on behalf of any other person must be deposited into the trust account unless all parties having an interest in the trust funds agree in writing to have the trust funds placed in a neutral escrow depository in Oregon. The principal broker must keep a true record of all trust funds passing through his hands, whether they are deposited in a trust account or in a neutral escrow depository.

An affiliated licensee must, within three banking days, transmit to his principal broker any money, checks, drafts, warrants, promissory notes or other consideration and any documents received in any professional real estate activity in which he is engaged. Failure to place earnest money in his principal broker's custody would be contrary to license law and cause for revocation of his license. Without the buyer's written instructions to the contrary, the affiliated licensee must transmit any earnest money to his principal broker within three banking days of receipt.

With certain exceptions, the principal broker must deposit funds belonging to others into a clients' trust account or a neutral escrow depository located in Oregon prior to the close of business of the fifth banking day following the date of receipt of the funds by any licensee working for him. A banking day is any day a financial institution is required to be open for the normal conduct of its business. It does not include Saturday, Sunday or any legal holiday. Therefore, whether earnest money was submitted to a broker on Friday or Saturday, it must be deposited in either a clients' trust account or a neutral escrow depository before the close of business Friday, since Monday, Tuesday, Wednesday, Thursday and Friday are the five banking days.

Note: *The broker has three banking days to get funds to the principal broker, so they may be deposited to the proper account within the five banking days from the time he received them. The deposit must be made by close of business of the fifth banking day, which could be 5:00 p.m., regardless of the time of day the funds were received.*

Funds need not be deposited within five banking days from receipt when the sales agreement states:
- the principal broker will hold an earnest money check undeposited until the offer is accepted or rejected and
- state where and when the check will be deposited after acceptance of the offer.

In this instance, the check must be deposited into the clients' trust account or deposited into escrow before the close of the third banking day following acceptance of the offer or a subsequent counteroffer.

Note, the following:
- Only earnest money may be held in this manner.
- Earnest money can only be held when it is in the form of a check. Cash, drafts and warrants must be deposited within five banking days of receipt.
- The sale agreement may call for the earnest money to be held until the offer is accepted or rejected. If the buyer wants it held for any other period, he should provide a note as earnest money.
- While the period for deposit of funds not held until acceptance of an offer is five banking days from receipt, the period for deposit of funds held until acceptance is three banking days from acceptance.

In addition, funds received need not be deposited at all if an offer is rejected before the deadline for depositing the check. Those funds may refunded without first being deposited and processed through the clients' trust account.

For all funds received, the principal broker must:
- account for the funds.
- maintain a copy of any check received.
- maintain a dated, acknowledged receipt for any check returned to the offeror.

Because a principal broker may place trust funds into a neutral escrow depository, many principal brokers do not have any clients' trust accounts. Instead, they write all offers directing that trust funds be immediately placed into escrow. A principal broker can place trust funds in a neutral escrow depository located in Oregon, only if all parties in the transaction agree in writing, and give instructions on how the escrow agent is to handle the funds.

The principal broker may not ever place funds into escrow or transfer funds from a clients' trust account into a neutral escrow agent on his own initiative. The escrow agent may accept funds, property or documents in an escrow transaction only with dated, written escrow instructions from the principals to the transaction or a dated executed agreement in writing between them, and the principal broker is not a principal to the transaction.

Generally, the instructions are included in the earnest money agreement. They indicate what the escrow agent is to do with the funds if the transaction is:
- consummated.
- terminated because of failure to satisfy contingencies.
- terminated because of default by the buyer.
- terminated because of default by the seller.

The escrow agent cannot close the escrow or disburse any funds or property in escrow without dated separate escrow instructions in writing from the principals, adequate to administer and close the transaction or to disburse the funds or property.

When the parties agree to have the funds placed in escrow, the funds must be placed there immediately. They are not deposited in the principal broker's clients' trust account. However, the principal broker must still account for the funds received by maintaining appropriate documentary evidence. His records must track the deposit from the buyer to the principal broker to the escrow depository.

For a transaction involving a real estate licensee holding an inactive license, all funds he receives in an offer or transaction would have to be placed into a neutral escrow depository, since he has no principal broker with a trust account.

In a cooperative transaction, when an offeror tenders an earnest money deposit in the form of cash or a check made payable to a selling principal broker, the selling principal broker must place the deposit in his clients' trust account.

After the seller accepts the offer and after receiving assurance that the earnest money deposit has cleared the bank, the selling principal broker can either:

- hold the funds until escrow is ready for them and then forward the funds to the escrow agent; or
- forward the deposit to the listing principal broker to be deposited into his clients' trust account, depending on the terms of the sales agreement.

If the deposit is in the form of a check made payable directly to the listing principal broker or escrow company as payee, the selling principal broker cannot deposit the check into his trust account. However, he must still maintain a record of receipt and disbursement of the funds.

When a deposit is tendered in the form of a promissory note, it should be payable to the seller, unless the parties agree otherwise. A note may be written to be redeemable upon acceptance, or within a specified period after acceptance, of the offer by the seller. The selling principal broker should hold the note until it is redeemed, and then return it to the buyer, obtain a receipt, and deposit the redeemed funds per the terms of the sale agreement.

As with other transactions, in a cooperative transaction the proposed purchaser and seller may agree to have the earnest money funds or note deposited with a neutral escrow. If the parties agree and provide the required escrow instructions, the cooperating principal broker can have the funds placed in a neutral escrow.

----- Disbursements -----

A check used to disburse funds from the clients' trust account must be prenumbered, issued from one numbering sequence, and bear the words "clients' trust account" on its face. A principal broker may not use any form of debit card on a clients' trust account.

Funds deposited into a clients' trust account and not disbursed or transferred to a neutral escrow depository as directed by the sale agreement may only be disbursed:

- to individuals, as directed by an order of the court;
- to individuals, as directed in writing by one or more principals; or
- to the court, upon filing, by the principal broker, of an interpleader action for disputed earnest money funds.

A principal broker cannot write checks on the trust account until a deposited check has cleared. If he deposits a $500 check and writes a check on the trust account the following day to refund the deposit and the check bounces, the trust account will be short of the amount of money it is supposed to have. This means money belonging to other clients will have been misspent to pay the buyer. That constitutes misuse of a client's funds. That is termed "conversion" and is illegal.

A principal broker must disburse earnest money from the trust account upon demand of the buyer, if:

- the buyer withdraws his offer and demands return of the money any time before acceptance of his offer by the seller is communicated to him.
- the seller makes a counteroffer which is refused, rejects the offer, or accepts the offer after the deadline imposed by the buyer for acceptance.
- after acceptance of the offer, the contingencies of the offer cannot be satisfied or the seller defaults.

The principal broker must also disburse earnest money and other consideration from the trust account upon demand of the buyer and without consent of the seller, if a buyer revokes his offer, based on disapproval of the Seller's Property Disclosure, and demands return of any deposits and other consideration, and:

- none of the buyers has waived the right of revocation;
- if the principal broker is closing the transaction, the buyer has not provided him with executed written instructions and executed documents necessary to close the transaction; and
- the buyer has provided him with a written release form and may provide indemnification against all liability arising from the return of all deposits and other consideration held by him in the transaction.
- the funds deposited into the trust account and credited to the buyer have been collected and are available for disbursement by the principal broker.

If a buyer defaults, the seller is entitled to the forfeited earnest money as liquidated damages. However, the forfeited earnest money will be disbursed to the seller and/or principal broker according to the agreement negotiated by the broker and seller at the time of executing the listing agreement or the earnest money agreement.

If the parties dispute ownership of the funds, the principal broker may disburse the disputed funds using procedures established by administrative rules or under the terms of a lawful contractual agreement. Funds are **disputed funds** when they have been deposited in the trust account under the terms of a written contract, and the parties to the contract dispute the disbursal of the funds. As soon as practicable after receiving a demand for the funds, the principal broker must send written notice to all parties that:

- a demand has been made and that the funds may be disbursed to the party who delivered the funds within 20 calendar days of the date of the demand, unless:
  - the parties deliver a written agreement regarding disbursal of the funds; or
  - one party provides proof to the principal broker within 20 calendar days of the date of the demand for disbursal that he has filed a legal claim to the funds.
- he has no legal authority to resolve questions of law or fact regarding disputed funds in the clients' trust account.
- disbursal of the funds will end his responsibility to account for the funds but will not affect any right or claim a person may have to the funds.
- both parties may wish to seek legal advice on the matter.

If the parties do not enter into a written agreement or neither party provides proof of filing a legal claim, the principal broker may disburse the funds to the person who delivered them within 20 calendar days of the date of the demand for disbursal. As an alternative, he may file an action to interplead the disputed funds. Under **interpleader**, the principal broker would just pay the disputed earnest money to the court and allow the court to determine how the disputed earnest money must be disbursed. Often, when the buyer and seller realize that the disputed funds will be reduced by the amount of court costs and attorney fees, they will settle the dispute without interpleader.

These requirements for dealing with disputes do not prevent the principal broker from:
- filing an action to interplead the disputed funds
- disbursing disputed funds based on:
  - the requirements of law.
  - the terms of the original sale agreement or any later agreement between the parties regarding the disbursal of funds

Maintenance of Records

----- TRUST ACCOUNT RECORDS -----

A principal broker must maintain a complete trust account ledger account and record of all funds received in his professional real estate activity. The ledger account must show:
- from whom the funds were received.
- the date they were received.
- the date they were deposited.
- where they were deposited.
- when the transaction has been completed or the offer has failed, the final disposition of the funds.

Every trust account deposit must be made with a deposit slip identifying each offer or transaction by a written notation of the file reference assigned to the offer or transaction. The principal broker must:
- account for all checks, including voided checks, as part of his records.
- record and track the transfer of promissory notes and other forms of consideration by a ledger account or other means (e.g., by written proof of transmittal or receipt retained in his offer or transaction file).
- record the transfer of other documents by written proof of transmittal or receipt retained in his offer or transaction file.

The principal broker must maintain a trust account **receipt and disbursement journal** or check register. A journal is a diary on which would appear an account of daily financial transactions. It will disclose the activity of deposits to and disbursements from the trust account, including:
- the date and amount of money received.
- from whom and for whom it was received.
- the identity of the property and/or the transaction or offer number.
- the date funds were deposited.
- the date funds were disbursed.
- the check number.
- to whom funds were disbursed.
- the purpose of the disbursement.

Below is the data for a sample check register:

> On January 3, 2005, a $1,000 earnest money check from John Morris was deposited to the trust account, creating a balance of $1,000 in the account. It was for the Simpson-Morris transaction. The transaction file number is 04-435.

> On January 4, 2005, a $2,000 earnest money check from Ron Jones was deposited to the trust account, creating a balance of $3,000 in the account. It was for the Smith-Jones transaction. The transaction file number is 04-436.

> On January 7, 2005, a $2,500 earnest money check from Mario Salsa was deposited to the trust account, creating a balance of $5,500 in the account. It was for the McKinsey-Salsa transaction. The transaction file number is 04-437.

> On January 9, 2005, a $1,500 earnest money check from Mike and Carol Barnes was deposited to the trust account as additional earnest money, creating a balance of $7,000 in the account. It was for the White-Barnes transaction. The transaction file number is 04-438.

> On January 10, 2005, a $10,000 earnest money check from the Sampson Corporation was deposited to the trust account, creating a balance of $17,000 in the account. It was for the Thompson-Sampson transaction. The transaction file number is 04-439.

> On January 21, 2005, a check (#1001) was written for a $1,000 commission to the principal broker, Sunnyview Realty, reducing the bank balance to $16,000. It was for the Simpson-Morris transaction. The transaction file number is 04-435.

> On January 23, 2005, a $1,500 earnest money check from Ron Jones was deposited to the trust account, creating a balance of $17,500 in the account. It was for the Smith-Jones transaction. The transaction file number is 04-436.

> On January 30, 2005, a $1,500 earnest money check from Gary Nisbaum was deposited to the trust account, creating a balance of $19,000 in the account. It was for the Taylor-Nisbaum transaction. The transaction file number is 04-440.

> On January 31, 2005, a $3,500 check (#1002) was written to American Title Co. reducing the balance to $15,500 in the account. It was for the Smith-Jones transaction. The transaction file number is 04-436.

> On February 1, 2005, a $2,000 earnest money check from Greg Marsh was deposited to the trust account, creating a balance of $17,500 in the account. It was for the Gregory-Marsh transaction. The transaction file number is 04-441.

> On February 1, 2005, a $1,000 earnest money check from Robert Wiley was deposited to the trust account, creating a balance of $18,500 in the account. It was for the Evergreen-Wiley transaction. The transaction file number is 04-442.

→On February 4, 2005, a $2,500 earnest money check from Lenny Miles was deposited to the trust account, creating a balance of $21,000 in the account. It was for the Haggerty-Miles transaction. The transaction file number is 04-443.

→On February 6, 2005, a $2,500 commission check (#1003) was written to Sunnyview Realty, reducing the balance to $18,500 in the account. It was for the McKinsey-Salsa transaction. The transaction file number is 04-437.

Date	File Number	Description of Transaction	Purpose	Debit (-)	Credit (+)	Balance
1/3/05	02-435	Simpson-Morris	Morris Em		$1,000.00	$1,000.00
1/4/05	02-436	Smith-Jones	Jones Em		$2,000.00	$3,000.00
1/7/05	02-437	McKinsey-Salsa	Salsa Em		$2,500.00	$5,500.00
1/9/05	02-438	White-Barnes	Barnes Em		$1,500.00	$7,000.00
1/10/05	02-439	Thompson-Sampson	Sampson Em		$10,000.00	$17,000.00
1/21/05	02-435	Simpson-Morris	SRE Comm	$1,000.00		$16,000.00
1/23/05	02-436	Smith-Jones	Jones Em		$1,500.00	$17,500.00
1/31/05	02-440	Taylor-Nisbaum	Nisbaum Em		$1,500.00	$19,000.00
1/31/05	02-436	Smith-Jones	AmeriTitle 1002	$3,500.00		$15,500.00
2/1/05	02-441	Gregory-Marsh	Marsh Em		$2,000.00	$17,500.00
2/1/05	02-442	Evergreen-Wiley	Wiley Em		$1,000.00	$18,500.00
2/4/05	02-443	Haggerty-Miles	Miles Em		$2,500.00	$21,000.00
2/6/05	02-437	McKinsey-Salsa	SRE Comm	$2,500.00		$18,500.00

If there is a large volume of entries being made, separate journals may be kept showing all cash receipts in one journal and all cash disbursements in the other.

In order for the principal broker to have an easy way of determining what has happened to the funds received on any particular offer or transaction, for at least each continuing account, he must maintain a **ledger account**. This is a separate current record for the deposits, withdrawals, and balances as taken from the journal, for a particular account. It shows the names of the payor and payee, the transaction number and property identification, and has columns to enter deposits, withdrawals and balances.

When funds are deposited in the clients' trust account, the deposit is recorded in the deposit column in both the journal and the individual ledger. The ledger entry should show the payor, the date of receipt, and the place and date of deposit. Any amount that is withdrawn from the trust account should be recorded in the journal and then entered in the individual client's ledger in the withdrawals column. The entry should include the check number, date, name of payee, and a brief description of the reason for the expenditure. When the transaction is completed or the offer has failed, the ledger should show final disposition of the funds. In order to assure that the accounts are maintained on a current basis at all times, entries from the journal should be posted to the proper ledger accounts daily.

The ledger below was created for the transaction involving the sale of the property at 12240 SE 16 St., Salem, OR 97301, by Al Smith to Ron Jones. It is transaction #04-436.

> → On January 2, 2005, the broker received a note for $2,000 as earnest money, payable within two days after acceptance of the offer. On January 4, the note was redeemed by Ron Jones with check #2135. The broker established the ledger for the transaction.
>
> → On January 29, 2005, Ron Jones gave the broker a $1,500 check (#2149) as additional earnest money, bringing the ledger balance to $3,500.
>
> → On January 31, 2005, the principal broker wrote a $3,500 check (#1002) to transfer the earnest money to American Title Company. This closed out the account.

ADDRESS: 1240 SE 16th Street			NAME: Smith-Jones		
Salem, Oregon 97301		TERMS:	LIMIT:	ACCT NO: 02-436	
DATE	ITEM	✓	DEBIT	CREDIT	BALANCE
1/2/05	$2,000 Em note				
	Due accept + 2 days				
1/4/05	Note redeemed			$2,000.00	$2,000.00
	Ron Jones ck. #2135				
1/29/05	Additional Em			$1,500.00	$3,500.00
	Ron Jones ck. #2149				
1/31/05	Transfer Em to Escrow		$3,500.00		$0
	AmeriTitle ck. #1002				

A broker must issue a **receipt** to evidence acceptance of funds or documents received and keep a copy of it in the transaction file. For earnest money deposits, the earnest money agreement itself serves as the necessary receipt, so no additional receipt is needed. The earnest money agreement must specify the amount and type of earnest money (check, note, property, etc.) received. When the broker receives cash or a check made payable to the principal broker's account as additional earnest money, as a rental payment or rental deposit, as payment on a contract, or when a note is redeemed, a receipt should be written.

Receipts used should be in duplicate so that one copy can be given to the payor and the other copy can be placed in the transaction file. They should also be prenumbered, to ensure that the money can be traced from receipt to deposit in the bank. Voided receipts should be retained and accounted for, just as voided checks would be, for this control to be effective. Each receipt should have written on it an explanation in sufficient detail so as to completely identify the item receipted for.

All deposits to the clients' trust account must be made with **deposit slips** furnished by the bank. Ideally, these slips should be filled out in duplicate, with one copy for the bank and one retained by the principal broker. If the copy is presented with the original deposit slip and deposit, it will be stamped by the bank teller and should be retained in the clients' trust account records. If the deposit is mailed, the deposit ticket returned by the bank should be stapled to the copy to which it applies. The bank deposit slip provides a convenient record to indicate the content of deposits to the trust account. The date of deposit of the trust funds can then be entered in the receipts and disbursements journal and the individual ledger.

A deposit slip must identify the transaction to which the funds apply by written notation of the consecutive file number assigned to the transaction and, as good practice, should show the number of the receipt given the payor. If the deposit is placed directly into escrow, a receipt should be obtained from the escrow or title company and kept on file.

CHECK & DEPOSIT INFORMATION IN DEAL FILE

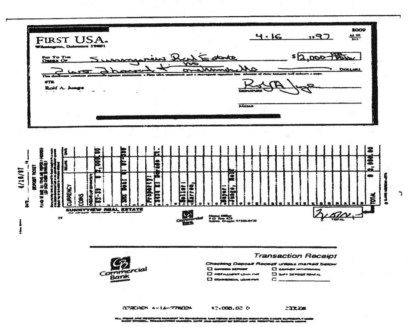

Any disbursement of trust funds must be made by prenumbered check drawn on the clients' trust account. The check must state "clients' trust account" on its face, identify the specific transaction or account by transaction number and describe the purpose of the check.

Afdsja Jfjaklfjlsa
Clients' Trust Account
1234 SW Main Street
Portland, OR 97123

10050

Date _____

Pay to the
 order of _____ $ _____

Bank of Realty
4321 SW Money Lane
Portland, OR 97432

Memo _____   _____

|: 3 2 5 0 7 0 7 6 0 |: 0 7 8 - 1 2 3 f 1 3 2 1 2 3 1 f

A disbursement from the trust account may be made only if the principal broker is authorized by law or written authorization of the parties in the transaction to do so. An earnest money agreement or management contract constitutes the authorization in most cases. Also, no funds may be disbursed on behalf of a client in excess of the balance in that client's account.

The bank will send a **statement of account** each month.

At least once each month, a principal broker must reconcile each clients' trust account. The reconciliation must have three components:

1. The bank statement balance, adjusted for outstanding checks and other reconciling bank items. Outstanding checks must be listed by check number, issue date, payee, and amount.
2. The balance of the receipts and disbursements journal or check book register as of the bank statement closing date
3. The sum of all the balances of the individual trust account ledgers as of the bank statement closing date

All three balances must be equal to and reconciled with each other. Any adjustment that may be needed must be clearly identified and explained.

Reconciliation is needed because the balance shown by the bank will not account for checks written which have not cleared the bank. The reconciliation is an explanation of the difference between the bank statement and the receipts and disbursements balance. The usual process is to review the checks returned by the bank and compare them with the record of disbursements. Checks written as of the date of the reconciliation which have not been returned by the bank will be reconciling factors, explaining some or all of the difference.

The principal broker must then document the reconciliation, showing that the reconciled bank balance equals both the sum of the clients' ledger accounts and the balance shown in the record of receipts and disbursements. He can use a reconciliation form developed by the Agency or the reverse of the statement provided by the bank. The Agency form instructs him to subtract the total amount of outstanding checks (checks written prior to the date of the statement, but which do not appear on the statement) from the bank's statement balance. Then he is to enter the account balance as shown in his records. If the result of the subtraction produces a figure equal to his account balance, the bank statement is reconciled. Aside from an occasional deposit in transit, which is handled in a similar manner, there should be no other reconciling factors.

The principal broker must:
- identify and promptly clear all reconciling items.
- verify, sign, and date the reconciliation when completed.
- preserve and file in logical sequence for at least six years:
    o the reconciliation worksheet
    o bank statements
    o all supporting documentation, including copies of the receipts and disbursements journal or check book register and a listing of each individual clients' trust fund account with a balance as of the reconciliation date. If these records are computerized, they must be printed out for filing with the reconciliation.

Real Estate Agency

1177 Center Street NE
Salem, Oregon 97301-2505
PHONE (503) 378-4170
FAX (503) 373-7153

**TRUST ACCOUNT
RECONCILIATION**

Trust Account Title

Sunnyview Real Estate

Client trust account

Date February 6, 2005

Prepared by John Doe

For month of January-05

Bank Commercial Bank, Salem, OR

Trust Acct No. 23350-05

PART I:

Bank Statement Balance on 01/31/05 $ 17,500.00

Plus: Deposits not yet credited to bank statement but posted to check
register and file ledgers   (Total of Schedule A) $ 1,500.00

Less: Outstanding checks. Checks written but not yet appearing on the
bank statement   (Total of Schedule B) $ 3,500.00

Plus or Minus: Account adjustments   (Total of Schedule C) $ 0.00

Reconciled bank balance as of 01/31/05   **PART I TOTAL *** $ 15,500.00

PART II:
Checkbook, Check Register or Journal of Receipts and disbursements

Balance as of 01/31/05   **PART II TOTAL *** $ 15,500.00

PART III:
Ledger card totals (Total of Schedule D)

Balance as of 01/31/05   **PART III TOTAL *** $ 15,500.00

PART IV
Reconciliation Summary - * Parts I, II and III must reconcile to the same date with the same amount.

Amount of difference in Totals of Parts I, II and III, if any $ 0.00

Explanation of differences and corrective action taken:

_____

_____

_____

_____

_____

_____

Reviewed by: John M. Doe   Date 1/31/05

NOTE: Trust accounts must be reconciled at least monthly. This form is utilized by Real Estate Agency auditors for trust
account reconciliations. It may be copied and utilized by real estate licensees if desired. Its use is not required.
91900-722 (Rev 1-01)

Schedules A-D

Schedule A (Deposits Not Yet Posted on Bank Statement)

Date	File #	Description	Amount
1/30/05	02-440	Taylor - Nisbaum	$ 1,500.00
			$ 0.00
TOTAL Schedule A (Enter here and in Part I of Reconciliation)			$ 1,500.00

Schedule B (Outstanding Checks)

Date	File #	Check #	Description	Amount
1/30/05	02-440	1002	Taylor - Nisbaum	$ 3,500.00
TOTAL Schedule B (Enter here and in Part I of Reconciliation)				$ 3,500.00

Schedule C (Other Adjustments)

Date	File #	Check #	Description	Amount
TOTAL Schedule C (Enter here and in Part I of Reconciliation)				

Schedule D (Ledger Cards)

File #	Description	Amount
02-437	McKinsey - Salsa	$ 2,500.00
02-438	White - Barnes	$ 1,500.00
02-439	Thompson - Sampson	$ 10,000.00
02-440	Taylor - Nisbaum	$ 1,500.00
TOTAL Schedule D (Enter here and in Part III of Reconciliation)		$ 15,500.00

NOTE: This form may be copied and utilized for lower volume accounts. For higher volume accounts, it may be necessary to prepare separate schedules.

Sunnyview Real Estate
RECONCILIATION DETAIL
Clients' Trust Account, Period Ending 1/31/05

TYPE	DATE	NUM	NAME	✓	AMOUNT	BALANCE
Beginning Balance						0
Cleared Transactions						
Checks and Payments – 1 item						
Check	1/21/05	1001	Sunnyview Real Estate	✓	-1,000.00	-1,000.00
Total Checks and Payments					-1,000.00	-1,000.00
Deposits and Credits – 6 items						
Deposit	1/3/05		John Morris	✓	1,000.00	1,000.00
Deposit	1/3/05		Ron Jones	✓	2,000.00	3,000.00
Deposit	1/3/05		Mario Salsa	✓	2,500.00	5,500.00
Deposit	1/3/05		Mike and Carol Burns	✓	1,500.00	7,000.00
Deposit	1/3/05		Sampson Corp.	✓	10,000.00	17,000.00
Deposit	1/3/05		Ron Jones	✓	1,500.00	18,500.00
Total Deposits and Credits					18,500.00	18,500.00
TOTAL CLEARED TRANSACTIONS					17,500.00	17,500.00
Cleared Balance					17,500.00	17,500.00
Uncleared Transactions						
Checks and Payments – 1 item						
Check	1/31/05	1002	Marsh		-3,500.00	-3,500.00
Total Checks and Payments					-3,500.00	-3,500.00
Deposits and Credits – 1 item						
Deposit	1/30/05		Nisbaum		1,500.00	1,500.00
Total Deposits and Credits					1,500.00	1,500.00
TOTAL UNCLEARED TRANSACTIONS					-2,000.00	-2,000.00
REGISTER BALANCE AS OF 1/31/05					15,500.00	15,500.00
New Transactions						
Checks and Payments – 1 item						
Check	2/6/05	1003	Sunnyview Real Estate		-2,500.00	-2,500.00
Total Checks and Payments					-2,500.00	-2,500.00
Deposits and Credits – 3 items						
Deposit	2/1/05		Greg Marsh		2,000.00	2,000.00
Deposit	2/1/05		Robert Wiley		1,000.00	1,000.00
Deposit	2/4/05		Lenny Miles		2,500.00	2,500.00
Total Deposits and Credits					5,500.00	5,500.00
TOTAL NEW TRANSACTIONS					3,000.00	3,000.00
Ending Balance					18,500.00	18,500.00

Sunnyview Real Estate
2/6/05

Date	Number	Name	Memo	Ref	Debit	✓	Credit	Balance
1/3/05		John Morris	Client funds in CTA	02-435		✓	1,000	1,000
1/4/05		Ron Jones	Client funds in CTA	02-436		✓	2,000	3,000
1/7/05		Mario Salsa	Client funds in CTA	02-437		✓	2,500	5,500
1/9/05		Mike & Carol Barnes	Client funds in CTA	02-438		✓	1,500	7,000
1/10/05		Sampson Corp.	Client funds in CTA	02-439		✓	10,000	17,000
1/21/05	1001	Sunnyview RE	Client funds in CTA	02-435	1,000	✓		16,000
1/23/05		Ron Jones	Client funds in CTA	02-436		✓	1,500	17,500
1/30/05		Nisbaum	Client funds in CTA	02-440			1,500	19,000
1/31/05	1002	AmeriTitle	Client funds in CTA	02-436	3,500			15,500
2/1/05		Greg Marsh	Client funds in CTA	02-441			2,000	17,500
2/1/05		Robert Wiley	Client funds in CTA	02-442			1,000	18,500
2/4/05		Lenny Miles	Client funds in CTA	02-443			2,500	21,000
2/6/05	1003	Sunnyview RE	Client funds in CTA	02-437	2,500			18,500

1:22 pm
2/6/05

Sunnyview Real Estate
CTA Balance Summary
Transactions with Balances

January 1-31, 2005

Clients' Trust Account

02-437 McKinsey to Salsa	2,500.00
02-438 White to Barnes	1,500.00
02-439 Thompson to Sampson	10,000.00
02-440 Taylor to Nisbaum	1,500.00
Total Clients' Trust Account Balance	15,500.00
TOTAL	15,500.00

Sunnyview Real Estate
CLIENTS' TRUST ACCOUNT DETAIL
January 1-31, 2005

02-435 Simpson-Morris							0
	1/3/05	Deposit	John Morris		✓	1,000.00	1,000.00
	1/21/05	Check	Sunnyview Real Estate	1001	✓	-1,000.00	-1,000.00
			Total 02-435 Simpson-Morris				**0.00**
02-436 Smith-Jones							
	1/4/05	Deposit	Ron Jones		✓	2,000.00	2,000.00
	1/23/05	Deposit	Ron Jones		✓	1,500.00	1,500.00
	1/31/05	Check	AmeriTitle	1002		-3.500.00	-3.500.00
			Total 02-436 Smith-Jones				**0.00**
02-437 McKinsey-Salsa							
	1/7/5	Deposit	Mario Salsa		✓	2,500.00	2,500.00
			Total 02-437 McKinsey-Salsa				**2,500.00**
02-438 White-Barnes							
	1/9/5	Deposit	Mike and Carol Barnes		✓	1,500.00	1,500.00
			Total 02-438 White-Barnes				**1,500.00**
02-439 Thompson-Sampson							
	1/9/05	Deposit	Sampson Corp.		✓	10,000.00	10,000.00
			Total 02-439 Thompson-Sampson				**10,000.00**
02-440 Taylor-Nisbaum							
	1/9/05	Deposit	Nisbaum		✓	1,500.00	1,500.00
			Total 02-440 Taylor-Nisbaum				**1,500.00**
			TOTAL CLIENTS' TRUST ACCOUNT				**15,000.00**

Brain Teaser

Reinforce your understanding of the material by correctly completing the following sentences:

1. If a branch office maintains a separate clients' trust account, it must also maintain a separate _____ system in the branch office.

2. An affiliated licensee must_____ transmit to his principal broker any money received in any professional real estate activity in which he is engaged.

3. Under _____, the principal broker would just pay the disputed earnest money to the court and allow the court to determine how the disputed earnest money must be disbursed.

4. A _____ account is a separate current record for the deposits, withdrawals, and balances as taken from the journal, for a particular account.

5. All real estate records, books, ledgers, bank statements, cancelled checks, and deposit slips must be maintained by the principal broker for at least _____ years.

Brain Teaser Answers

1. If a branch office maintains a separate clients' trust account, it must also maintain a separate **bookkeeping** system in the branch office.

2. An affiliated licensee must **promptly** transmit to his principal broker any money received in any professional real estate activity in which he is engaged.

3. Under **interpleader**, the principal broker would just pay the disputed earnest money to the court and allow the court to determine how the disputed earnest money must be disbursed.

4. A **ledger** account is a separate current record for the deposits, withdrawals, and balances as taken from the journal, for a particular account.

5. All real estate records, books, ledgers, bank statements, cancelled checks, and deposit slips must be maintained by the principal broker for at least **six** years.

Review – Oregon Trust Accounts

This lesson covers broker responsibility for trust funds, trust accounts and recordkeeping.

Every sole principal broker or principal broker will keep a general checking account as his operating account, to handle funds that belong to the brokerage firm. Unless he always places trust funds in a neutral escrow depository, he must maintain in Oregon at least one separate bank account designated as a clients' trust account. This is a bank checking account or an interest-bearing savings account into which the broker must deposit all trust funds received or handled by him or his licensees on behalf of any other person, except for those funds immediately placed in escrow.

A broker may have any number of clients' trust accounts. If a branch office maintains a separate clients' trust account, it must also maintain a separate bookkeeping system in the branch office. A broker may place trust funds in an interest-bearing bank account, if it is federally insured and designated a clients' trust account and if he has the prior written authorization of all parties having an interest in the trust funds.

The broker must, on forms approved by the Real Estate Commissioner (the Commissioner), identify to the Real Estate Agency (the Agency) the name of the bank, the account number and the name of the account for each clients' trust account he maintains, and provide the Commissioner with authorization to examine the accounts.

Commingling

Clients' funds must be placed in a clients' trust account or neutral escrow depository in order to assure there is no commingling of licensee funds with client funds. A broker is required to place funds in the clients' trust account or escrow relating to the sale of property owned by himself or owned by licensees working for him in order to protect parties dealing with the licensee. This does not apply to rental transactions of licensee-owned property, unless the brokerage is managing the property and charging a fee for bookkeeping, management or collection of funds.

Deposits

All trust funds received or handled by the broker, or by any licensee associated with him, on behalf of any other person must be deposited into the clients' trust account unless all parties having an interest in the trust funds agree in writing to have the trust funds placed in a neutral escrow depository in Oregon.

An affiliated licensee must promptly transmit to his principal broker any money, checks, drafts, warrants, promissory notes or other consideration and any documents received in any professional real estate activity in which he is engaged within 3 banking days. With certain exceptions, the principal broker must deposit funds belonging to others into a clients' trust account or a neutral escrow depository located in Oregon prior to the close of business of the fifth banking day following the date of receipt of the funds by any licensee working for him. When a sales agreement states that the broker will hold an earnest money check undeposited until the offer is accepted, and further states where and when the check will be deposited after acceptance of the offer, the check must be deposited into the clients' trust account or deposited into escrow before the close of the third banking day following mutual acceptance of the offer or a subsequent counter offer.

A broker can place trust funds in a neutral escrow depository located in Oregon only if all parties in the transaction agree in writing and give instructions on how the escrow agent is to handle the funds.

When a deposit is tendered in the form of a promissory note, it should be payable to the seller, unless the parties agree otherwise.

Disbursements

Any check used to disburse funds from the clients' trust account must be prenumbered and bear the words "clients' trust account" on its face. If a buyer defaults, forfeited earnest money will be disbursed to the seller and/or broker according to the agreement negotiated by the broker and seller at the time of executing the listing agreement or the earnest money agreement.

Records

A broker must maintain a complete record of all funds, promissory notes or other consideration received in his professional real estate activity. Every trust account deposit must be made with a deposit slip identifying each offer or transaction by a written notation of the file number assigned to the offer or transaction.

A trust account receipt and disbursement journal is a diary on which would appear an account of daily financial transactions. In order for the broker to have an easy way of determining what has happened to the funds received on any particular offer or transaction, for at least each continuing account, he must maintain a ledger account. This is a separate current record for the deposits, withdrawals, and balances as taken from the journal, for a particular account.

All deposits to the clients' trust account must be made with deposit slips furnished by the bank. A deposit slip must identify the transaction to which the funds apply by written notation of the consecutive file number assigned to the transaction and, as good practice, should show the number of the receipt given the payor. Any disbursement of trust funds must be made by prenumbered check drawn on the clients' trust account which states "clients' trust account" on its face, identifies the specific transaction or account by transaction number and describes the purpose of the check.

Each month the record of receipts and disbursements must be reconciled with the ledger accounts and the bank statement, as of the ending date of the balance on the bank statement. All real estate records, books, ledgers, bank statements, cancelled checks, and deposit slips must be maintained by the broker for at least six years.